NEW VEGETARIAN

NEW VEGETARIAN

MORE THAN 75 FRESH, CONTEMPORARY RECIPES FOR
PASTA, TAGINES, CURRIES, SOUPS AND STEWS, AND DESSERTS

BY ROBIN ASBELL

PHOTOGRAPHS BY YVONNE DUIVENVOORDEN

CHRONICLE BOOKS
SAN FRANCISCO

Library of Congress Cataloging-in-Publication Data available.

ISBN 978-0-8118-6579-1

Manufactured in China

Designed by Patrick Nistler
Prop styling by Catherine Doherty
Food styling by Lucie Richard

Sriracha Sauce is a registered trademark of V. Thai Food Product Co., Ltd;
Huy Fong Foods, Inc.; Tabasco is a registered trademark of McIlhenny Co.; Thai
Kitchen Curry Paste is a registered trademark of Epicurian International Inc.

10 9 8 7 6 5 4 3 2

Chronicle Books LLC
680 Second Street
San Francisco, California 94107
www.chroniclebooks.com

Many thanks

This book was born with the unswerving support of my sweetheart, Stan, who has tasted every vegetarian recipe with me for 26 years. My family and friends have made the creative journey fun.

I want to thank Sarah Billingsley, Amy Treadwell, Peter Perez, Anne Donnard, Doug Ogan, David Hawk, and the whole creative team at Chronicle. Yvonne Duivenvoorden and the food photography crew did a wonderful job bringing the food to life.

My IACP and Greenbrier friends and colleagues all contributed to this book, in ways great and small. Special thanks to John Ash and Yukari Sakamoto for informing the umami broth recipe, and to everyone who gave me ideas and support. All my magazine editors and cooking school directors also deserve thanks, as they keep me on my toes.

To my special client family, I hope you know how much it means to me that you like the food.

TABLE OF CONTENTS

INTRODUCTION

EAT YOUR VEGETABLES

It's too bad that we have to differentiate between vegetarian food and food in general, because it seems that once we call something "vegetarian," or even worse, "healthy," there is a large group of people who won't even try it. In this book, I share dishes that I have served to passionately omnivorous people who enjoyed them thoroughly. In fact, when these dishes were served alongside the meat dishes that my guests were certain they preferred, the plant-based specialties were devoured and raved about.

After watching the vegetarian option disappear first over and over again at gatherings I attended or catered, I was moved to put together a collection of recipes that any vegetarian can take to a feast where omnivores are present. Each savory recipe makes something that can stand in as a complete vegetarian meal, just as it can—and will be—shared by everyone. The desserts are vegan, but attractive and delicious enough to lure the most committed junk foodist.

A vegetarian diet is no longer uncommon in our communities. In fact, there's a good chance that someone in your family or circle of friends is a vegetarian. But if you're the only one, bringing great food and living well are probably the best ways to convince your loved ones that you are making the right food choices.

Eating a meatless diet is not new. Over the centuries, many groups of people have practiced vegetarianism, from Buddhists and Brahmans to Seventh-day Adventists. Pythagorus, Aristotle, and Leonardo da Vinci were celeb veggies, proving that you don't need meat to be smart. Of course, Hitler was a vegetarian, too, so it's no guarantee.

In centuries past, a population's meat intake was usually limited by economics and the environment, and everybody ate what we would call "vegetarian" meals as a matter of course. Before giant factory farms kept our supermarkets and fast-food places stocked with cheap meat, folks simply had less access to it. The standard American diet is unhealthful for many reasons, not the least of which is too much factory-farmed meat.

There are many reasons for going veg. During a vegetarian's lifetime, one can switch from one reason to the next and never run out. One reason that is taking on new urgency today is the environment. In 2006 the Food and Agriculture Organization of the United Nations released the report "Livestock's Long Shadow," in which the global impact of raising animals for food was assessed. It turns out that livestock, and all the activities involved in the meat-making industry, produce 18 percent of the greenhouse gases emitted per year—beating out transportation as a source of global warming.

Between 1970 and 2002, developing countries' meat consumption per capita increased from 24 to 64 pounds, and in developed nations like our own, from 143 to 176 pounds. A person who eats meat is responsible for 1.5 tons more carbon dioxide per year than a vegetarian. A person following a low-fat vegetarian diet needs less than half (0.44) an acre per person per year to produce his or her food, while a typical meat eater needs 2.11 acres. This means that more forests must be cleared for raising animals, which is a leading cause of the destruction of rain forests. A vegetarian who shops locally can reduce his or her carbon footprint that much more.

Another good reason to drop meat is for the benefit of your health. Vegetarians are typically healthier than the rest of the population and avoid many of the diet-related diseases of our times. Eliminating meat cuts saturated fat and cholesterol and, almost as important, makes room for more protective foods. It may well be that plant-based foods are so loaded with good things that we live longer just by eating more veggies instead of filling up on beef. Replacing meat with beans and soy adds antioxidants and fiber and lowers cholesterol instead of raising it. Grass-fed cows and chicken produce dairy and eggs that contain the same good fats that are in fish, as well as vitamin B-12. Filling up on veggies floods your body with cancer-preventing, cleansing chemicals instead of hindering it with slowly digesting flesh foods.

Studying the effects of diet is tricky because so many factors influence disease. In the Adventist Health Study, vegetarian men had 38 percent lower rates of heart disease and lived 3.21 more years than nonvegetarian men. Vegetarian women lived 2.52 years longer. Overall, vegetarians had half the high blood pressure, diabetes, and colon cancer, and two-thirds the rheumatoid arthritis and prostate cancer. In general, folks who ate vegetarian, ate nuts regularly, exercised, and kept their weight down were the healthiest. Doctors like Dean Ornish and John McDougall have long track records of reversing heart disease and many other serious ailments with vegetarian diets. Vegetarians who also choose a lot of other healthful habits— like not smoking, not drinking in excess, exercising, and eating lots of whole grains, fruits, and veggies—greatly improve their chances of a longer, healthier life.

Another benefit of avoiding meat products is that you avoid the growing problems with unsafe food handling. Large-scale meat production and the risks of bacterial contamination go together, and it is increasingly common for meats to be the cause of food poisoning. The possibility of diseases like mad cow and bird flu devastating this country, as they have others, is very real.

The third major reason that people go vegetarian is to avoid the suffering and death of other living beings. Most of the organized groups of vegetarians, like Buddhists, practice vegetarianism for spiritual reasons. Whether you believe in Karma and reincarnation, or just in compassion and peace, taking lives unnecessarily may not feel right. In today's factory farms and slaughterhouses, animals live short lives that are very different from any natural life they might have had, ending in fear and pain. Vegetarians don't participate in the process.

HOW VEGETARIANISM IS PRACTICED

OVO-LACTO: WHAT MOST PEOPLE THINK OF WHEN YOU SAY "VEGETARIAN"

For the ovo-lacto vegetarian, as long as no animal dies for the food, it's okay to consume. Milking a cow or taking eggs from a chicken are ways to eat animal proteins without taking a life. From a nutritional standpoint, cutting out meat while keeping eggs and dairy helps to lower the amount of saturated fat in the diet. Ovo-lactos don't have to make as much of an effort to get calcium, iron, and B-12 as vegans do, because dairy and eggs provide them. A healthful ovo-lacto diet will also include beans, nuts and seeds, and soy foods to balance the animal products.

VEGAN: PURELY VEGETARIAN

The vegan goes a step further, giving up any product that comes from a living creature—so eggs, dairy, and honey are off the list. Beyond the kitchen, leather, fur, and other animal parts are avoided. Depending on the vegan's devotion to the practice, cutting out hidden animal products in everyday household goods can be challenging. For example, the film in nondigital cameras contains gelatin, some food colorings are made from insects, and multitudes of things you would never suspect have tiny amounts of both slaughterhouse and dairy derivatives. About 15 percent of the white cane sugar sold is purified with charcoal made from cow bones, so serious vegans use other sweeteners, unrefined sugar, or beet sugar.

Vegans have no cholesterol or saturated fat in their diets. They do need to be careful that they include enough of the vegetarian sources of B vitamins, iron, calcium, and other nutrients found in animal foods.

FLEXITARIAN

I'm betting that most of you reading this book are flexitarian and probably don't know it. This title was invented to describe folks who eat a lot of vegetarian food, but when the moment suits them, they eat meat or fish. The world at large, especially abroad, defines vegetarianism as not eating visible chunks of beef, pork, or chicken—but going ahead with fish, meat stocks and sauces, and shrimp paste is okay. Pescatarians are another form of flexitarian, because fish are not vegetables—and they're not red or white meat, either. People are free to make their food choices however they see fit. It's not black and white; anyone who adds some veggie meals to his or her diet will benefit and will help the environment by cutting back on greenhouse gases.

WHOLE FOODS

There are as many ways to be a vegetarian as there are vegetarians. We all make decisions based on taste, availability, nutrition, and cost. Still, if there is one idea that should attach to the vegetarian label automatically, it is the whole-foods approach. At its most basic, it is the practice of looking for foods that are as unrefined and natural as possible. Sticking to real foods is smart. Human beings ate real foods for thousands of years before we got into food chemistry. Our bodies work best with whole foods, not assemblages of parts of foods held together with high fructose corn syrup and preservatives.

Thinking whole foods while shopping and preparing meals will guide you to choose whole-grain products over white, oil and vinegar over bottled fat-free concoctions, and real tofu over light tofu bologna. As you will read in the following pages, vegetarians, especially vegans, need to eat almost exclusively whole grain, with copious amounts of dark leafy greens, vegetables, nuts and seeds, and beans in order to get the nutrients they need. Giving up meat is just part of the healthful veg diet—it has to be replaced with the most nutrient-dense plant foods to create the kind of vibrant health you want. Just because potato chips and beer are vegetarian doesn't make them a nutritious dinner.

HOW TO GET YOUR PROTEIN AND OTHER NUTRIENTS

The Protein Myth is so ingrained in us that the first thing family and friends will ask a newly declared vegetarian is how they will get their protein. The fact is, protein is easy to find. A head of Romaine lettuce has 106 calories and 8 grams of protein. Eat six of them and you get 636 calories and 48 grams of protein, all the protein a 132-pound person needs in a day. Nobody is recommending that as a diet, but it illustrates that as long as you are eating adequate calories of natural, healthful foods, the fabled protein problem almost takes care of itself.

Here are two very basic menus that include protein. With minimal effort, each meal plan exceeds an adult's protein needs, while amassing fewer than 2,000 calories.

A DAY OF PROTEIN FOR A VEGAN

BREAKFAST:
1 cup cooked oatmeal / 6 G PROTEIN
1 cup soy milk / 5 G PROTEIN
1 banana / 1 G PROTEIN

LUNCH:
One 6-inch whole wheat pita / 6 G PROTEIN
½ cup hummus / 10 G PROTEIN
1 small green salad with ½ cup sunflower seeds / 15 G PROTEIN
1 stalk broccoli / 7 G PROTEIN

DINNER:
1 cup black bean soup / 14 G PROTEIN
½ cup cooked quinoa / 11 G PROTEIN
½ cup cooked carrots / 1 G PROTEIN
1 cup cooked spinach / 5 G PROTEIN
One 1.5-ounce chocolate bar with almonds / 4 G PROTEIN

TOTAL GRAMS OF PROTEIN: 85
TOTAL CALORIES: 1,987

A DAY OF PROTEIN FOR AN OVO-LACTO

BREAKFAST:
⅔ cup low-fat granola / 4 G PROTEIN
1 cup fat-free yogurt / 14 G PROTEIN
1 banana / 1 G PROTEIN

LUNCH:
2 slices whole wheat bread / 8 G PROTEIN
2 ounces chèvre cheese / 10 G PROTEIN
1 cup roasted eggplant and red peppers / 1 G PROTEIN

DINNER:
1 cup cooked brown rice / 5 G PROTEIN
1 teaspoon sesame oil / 0 G PROTEIN
1 cup cooked spinach / 5 G PROTEIN
1 cup cooked broccoli / 2 G PROTEIN
1 cup napa cabbage / 2 G PROTEIN
½ cup sliced carrot / 2 G PROTEIN
1 cup edamame / 17 G PROTEIN
2 tablespoons teriyaki sauce / 2 G PROTEIN

TOTAL GRAMS OF PROTEIN: 70
TOTAL CALORIES: 1,547

B VITAMINS

Unlike protein, vitamin B-12 does require some effort to obtain, especially if you are vegan. B vitamins are actually the bacteria vitamins, made by bacteria that live in the soil and in animal guts. In days past, we could have gotten our B-12 by eating dirt on carelessly washed fresh produce, drinking water from streams and ponds, and from other unsanitary practices. These days, we treat our water and wash our produce to avoid illness from bad bacteria, but our bodies still need what they got from the old environment. The lack of B-12 in vegetables is not proof that we need meat, just that we used to be less sanitary in our habits, and we don't have to take those risks now. Instead of taking in all the bacteria in pond water and hoping for the best, we can grow bacteria that produce vitamin B-12 and harvest it, then add it to our food.

In light of this, many cereals, soy milks, and vegetarian foods have been fortified with vitamin B-12. Depending on the brand, you may get your entire day's worth of B-12 from a bowl of fortified cereal and a cup of fortified soy milk. Red Star nutritional yeast is grown on a B-12-rich medium to give it 25 percent of the daily need per tablespoon. You'll see small amounts of this nutritional yeast in vegan recipes throughout this book. Feel free to sprinkle it on salads and into salad dressings and soups, or add to popcorn for a snack.

The other B vitamins are less of a conundrum, and vegetable eaters actually get more than anyone else if they regularly eat leafy greens and whole grains.

IRON AND ZINC

The iron in vegetables, called nonheme iron, differs from the heme iron in meat and is harder for the body to absorb. Plant foods like dark leafy greens, beans, nuts and seeds, and sea vegetables have lots of nonheme iron. The iron is better absorbed when vitamin C–containing foods are consumed with them, and it is best to have tea or red wine at a different time, because the tannins inhibit absorption. Cook your food in cast-iron pans and you will add iron effortlessly. Zinc is in many of the same foods as iron, so eating nuts, seeds, whole grains, beans, and tofu will keep your levels up.

CALCIUM

Ovo-lactos have an easy time ingesting sufficient calcium. Vegans may need to seek out fortified soy milks and eat lots of leafy greens. Dark green vegetables, nuts and seeds, beans, and sea veggies all provide calcium.

VITAMIN D

The sunshine vitamin, D is a crucial player in remineralizing your bones. If you get 15 minutes of daytime sun on your face and hands if you have fair skin, or 30 minutes if you have dark skin, you will get enough D. If not, fortified dairy and soy milks will probably give you the necessary 5 micrograms needed for folks under age 50, going up to 10 micrograms for those over 50. Vitamin D-2 is the vegetarian form of D made from yeast, and it is necessary to take more of it, as it is not as well absorbed.

VITAMIN E AND TRACE MINERALS

Go with whole grains, and you will be replacing all of the E and trace minerals that are missing from the American diet. Mix it up—part of the fun and nutrition of a veg diet is varying the foods you eat. Whole wheat bread is great, but branching out to eat rye, millet, or black rice will add nutrients and variety.

PHYTOCHEMICALS

New antioxidants are still being discovered and studied, and all of them are in plant foods. Cancer-preventing, cell-protecting elements are stuffed into the veggies, fruits, grains, beans, nuts, seeds, and even herbs and spices we eat. Strive to get nine servings of vegetables and fruits a day in a variety of colors, and you will be bathing your cells in good phytochemicals.

ESSENTIAL FATTY ACIDS (EFA)

Omega-6 and omega-3 fats are the reason people take fish oil capsules, but you don't have to. Among other things, these fats are crucial to brain and nerve functions. Vegetarians typically do well with the omega-6s, linoleic acid, gamma-linoleic acid, and arachidonic acids (LA, GLA, and AA). AA is largely from animal foods and is associated with heart disease and inflammation, so keeping it low is good. Linoleic acid is in nuts, seeds and their oils, grains, and soybean oil, all of which are usually prevalent in a veg diet, so there's not usually a deficiency here. The omega-3s are where vegetarians and especially vegans can have trouble. Alpha-linoleic acid (ALA), found in flax, hemp, walnut, and canola oils, as well as in green leafy vegetables and sea vegetables, is the easiest of the 3s to encounter. But the eicosapentaenoic and docosahexaenoic acids (EPA and DHA) that come from fish, from the algae that fish eat, or from sea vegetables are harder to get in a veg lifestyle. Vegetarian supplements made from algae are available now, and vegans would be wise to consider supplementing, as well as adding freshly ground flaxseeds to their diets. GLA is in evening primrose oil, borage oil, hemp oil, and spirulina.

Bear in mind that the body converts some of the LA you consume into GLA and AA, and the ALA into EPA and DHA, as long as you consume adequate amounts and don't overdo the omega-6s, which puts the system out of balance.

Fats are crucial to the absorption of other nutrients as well, so don't go fat-free.

Another thing for ovo-lactos to keep in mind is the superiority of grass-fed animal fats. As we know with fish that eat algae, cows that eat grass produce better balances of EFAs in their own body fats. That means that milk, cheese, and butter from grass-fed cows have those "green source" fats, instead of corn- and grain-sourced. Studies show that grass-fed dairy is 3 to 5 times higher in omega-3s and conjugated linoleic acid, which is sold as a supplement to prevent cancer and lose weight. Chickens who scratch in pasture, eating plants and bugs, also produce better fat balances in their eggs, which contain more nutrients, like the carotenoids that make the yolks vibrant orange. A side benefit is that the animals are happier and healthier, as well!

SOURCE GUIDE FOR UNUSUAL INGREDIENTS

While it's always best to support local shops, for those who live outside of urban centers, the offerings can be slim. Luckily, with the Internet, the more obscure and specialized ingredients can be just a click away!

BOB'S RED MILL NATURAL FOODS / *www.bobsredmill.com*
Specializing in nearly 400 different types of natural, organic, or gluten-free whole grains, flours, meals, masa harina, beans, and seeds. Bob's Red Mill products are available in many supermarkets nationwide or online at the Web site.

E-FOOD DEPOT / *www.efooddepot.com*
This Web site can be searched by ingredient or by region. Hard-to-find ingredients available here include palm sugar and seeds, nori, curry paste, and wasabi, as well as certain types of peas, rice, and noodles.

EDEN FOODS / *www.edenfoods.com/store*
Selling traditional Japanese ingredients such as matcha, shoyu, ume plum concentrate, and miso, Eden Foods also offers pasta, whole grains, kamut flakes, teas, and beans all grown organically and produced in a sustainable manner.

ETHNIC GROCER / *www.ethincgrocer.com*
A sort of one-stop online shop for various ethnic ingredients. The Web site can be searched by ingredient, like kombu or yuzu, or by geographic regions.

FIRST FOOD / *www.firstfood.com*
Mock duck, mock abalone, and other meatless products are available, in addition to Asian mushrooms, noodles, sauces, and picked ginger.

IMPORT FOOD / *www.importfood.com*
Offers Thai and Japanese ingredients, including tamarind pulp, chili sauces, mirin, dried seaweed, oils, Sriracha, dried lemongrass, specialty sugars, rice and tapioca flours, and even fresh produce.

KOA MART / *www.koamart.com*
Sells tofu (in blocks and noodles), udon, soy milk, many types of seaweed, umeboshi, kimchi, condiments, spices, and many dried Asian specialty ingredients.

PENZEY'S SPICES / *www.penzeys.com*
One of the most famous vendors of herbs and spices in the nation. Penzey's also sells premixed spice blends suitable for use as marinades or more complex flavorings for all dishes. There are also a considerable number of salt-free spice mixes and blends.

SHAMRA / *www.shamra.com*
Middle Eastern online shop selling gourmet foods from tahini and pomegranate syrup to grape leaves and bulgur wheat.

THAI KITCHEN / *www.worldpantry.com*
Offering Thai specialty ingredients, including chili sauces, curry pastes, and specialty rice and noodles.

URBAN HERBS / *www.urbanherbs.com*
Selling spices, herbs, rice, grains, beans, and even sugar, Urban Herbs offers ingredients from mainstream to exotic at affordable prices online or at their retail store in Cleveland.

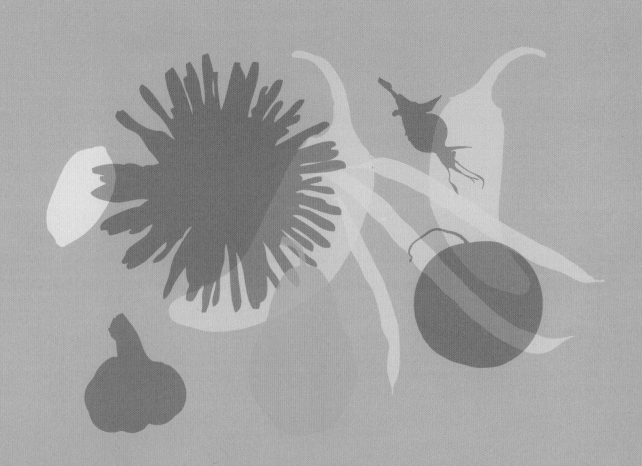

CHAPTER 1

APPETIZERS AND LIGHT MEALS

THE APPETIZER IS TYPICALLY SERVED IN TWO SETTINGS.
It can be a small course, served as a warm-up to the rest of the meal, or it can be a party nosh, served with drinks. All of the appetizers in this chapter will delight your friends in either role and can even be served as light entrees.

A spread of appetizers is usually friendly-but-boring territory for a vegetarian, since people often serve meatless things like crackers and crudités.

If you lay out a platter of these exciting, beautiful vegetarian appetizers, the other apps will pale in comparison. Offering to bring an appetizer is a generous gesture that has the side benefit of making sure the vegs have something to eat. These recipes make irresistible finger food for everyone; just make sure the vegetarians get some before they disappear.

The art of the appetizer lies in making little bites of deliciousness that complement the food to follow or the drinks at hand. Crispy, bite-size croquettes, flaky phyllo-wrapped goodies, tender dumplings, and good things rolled up in wrappers fill the bill. Dipping sauces put their appeal over the top. To go with all of your Asian meals, many of these apps are Asian influenced, and all of them will convince the meat-lovers that you really know how to live!

FRENCH LENTIL CROQUETTES

with MINT AIOLI

MAKES ABOUT 12 CROQUETTES / SERVES 4

These crispy croquettes are delicious with a garlicky-mint mayonnaise or simply dipped in Dijon mustard. It's a fun way to dress up our favorite legume, and it's fit for a party. Don't use extra-virgin olive oil for the aioli, since it contains acids that can break the emulsifying abilities of the yolks and ruin your dip.

INGREDIENTS

½ CUP PUY *or* FRENCH LENTILS

1 LARGE EGG

1 CLOVE GARLIC,
crushed

2 TABLESPOONS MINCED FRESH THYME

¾ TEASPOON SALT

¼ TEASPOON PEPPER

¾ CUP DRY BREADCRUMBS
(panko is best)

1 TABLESPOON OLIVE OIL

MINT AIOLI

1 CLOVE GARLIC,
peeled

1 LARGE EGG YOLK

1 TABLESPOON LEMON JUICE

¼ TEASPOON SALT

1 PINCH CAYENNE PEPPER

½ CUP CANOLA *or* LIGHT OLIVE OIL
(not extra-virgin olive oil)

½ CUP MINCED FRESH MINT

1 Put the lentils and 4 cups of water in a pot over high heat. Bring to a boil, reduce the heat to a simmer, and cover. Simmer until tender but not mushy, about 30 minutes. Drain and cool. Mix the lentils with the egg, garlic, thyme, salt, pepper, and ½ cup of the breadcrumbs. Mash with your hands until the mixture holds together.

2 Form heaping tablespoons of the mixture into small patties, coat with the remaining breadcrumbs, and chill.

3 In a medium saute pan over medium heat, heat the olive oil. Add the lentil patties and fry until golden, 3 to 5 minutes on each side. Serve hot with the aioli.

4 **To make the aioli:** In a food processor, mince the garlic until finely chopped. Add the yolk, lemon juice, salt, and cayenne and purée to mix. Gradually drizzle in the oil while the machine is running. Add the minced mint and pulse to mix. Makes ½ cup aioli.

INSIDE-OUT JICAMA-TOFU ROLLS

Wrapped in MANGO with GINGER SAUCE

MAKES 8 ROLLS

A tropical draping of mango makes these light rolls the height of summer food fun.
You will need a mandoline or slicing box for the mangoes and a makisu, or sushi-rolling mat,
for making rolls. If you want an easier option, coat the rolls with toasted sesame seeds.

INGREDIENTS

3 CUPS SUSHI RICE
washed and drained

3 TABLESPOONS RICE VINEGAR

1½ TABLESPOONS SUPERFINE SUGAR

10 OUNCES FIRM TOFU,
drained and pressed

1 TABLESPOON DARK SESAME OIL

2 TABLESPOONS TERIYAKI SAUCE

8 SHEETS NORI

½ SMALL JICAMA,
cut into sticks

1 MEDIUM CARROT,
cut into long, thin strips

8 TEASPOONS UME PLUM PASTE

8 TEASPOONS MAYONNAISE
(optional)

4 LARGE FIRM RIPE MANGOES

GINGER SAUCE

¼ CUP FRESHLY GRATED FRESH GINGER,
about 4 inches of root

¼ CUP HONEY OR SUGAR

¼ CUP SOY SAUCE

PICKLED GINGER

1 In a pot over high heat, bring 3¾ cups of water and the rice to a boil, cover tightly, and reduce heat to low. Simmer, covered, until all of the water is absorbed, 10 to 15 minutes. Let stand, covered, for at least 5 minutes.

2 Heat the vinegar and sugar together in a small saucepan to dissolve the sugar. Pour the mixture over the rice and fold it in with a rice paddle. Fan the rice to cool it and cover with a wet kitchen towel.

3 Preheat the oven to 400°F. Slice tofu into sticks, then spread the sesame oil on a sheet pan. Put the tofu on the oil and drizzle with the teriyaki sauce, gently coating the tofu. Bake for 20 minutes. Let cool.

4 Wrap a sushi-rolling mat with plastic wrap. Place a sheet of nori on the mat and spread about ¾ cup of the rice over the entire sheet. Carefully turn over rice-covered nori on the mat. In the center of the nori sheet, place a tofu stick, some jicama and carrot, and dab on 1 teaspoon of ume paste and 1 teaspoon of mayonnaise (if using). Keep the fillings in place with your fingers as you roll, enclosing the fillings. Lightly shape the finished roll in the mat.

5 Use a mandoline to slice very thin sheets of mango. On a sheet of plastic wrap, place enough sliced mango to cover a roll. Blot the surface of the fruit with a kitchen towel. Place a roll on the mango slices with the seam side down and pull up the plastic. Gently stick the mango to the surface. Slice each roll into 6 pieces, leaving the plastic wrap on, then remove the wrap.

6 **To make the ginger sauce:** Stir the ginger, honey, and soy sauce in a small bowl. Place the rolls on their sides, mango-side up, drizzled with the sauce. Garnish with pickled ginger and serve.

KIMCHI DUMPLINGS

with PINE NUT DIPPING SAUCE

MAKES 24 DUMPLINGS / SERVES 4

The filling for these dumplings is so simple and fast, it makes dumpling cuisine easy. Kimchi stars as an instant flavor-packed precooked veggie, and the tofu balances the heat of the spicy cabbage perfectly.

INGREDIENTS

1 CUP KIMCHI,
drained and chopped

½ PACKAGE EXTRA-FIRM TOFU,
pressed

2 TABLESPOONS CHOPPED FRESH GINGER

2 SCALLIONS,
chopped

1 TEASPOON CORNSTARCH

½ TEASPOON SALT

24 ROUND GYOZA WRAPPERS

PINE NUT DIPPING SAUCE

1 TABLESPOON PINE NUTS

½ CUP SOY SAUCE

1 TEASPOON CHILI-INFUSED SESAME OIL

¼ TEASPOON SUGAR

1 CLOVE GARLIC,
crushed

1 Set up your steamer and either oil the steamer basket or plate you will steam the dumplings on or cut little pieces of parchment paper for the dumplings.

2 In a large bowl, mix the kimchi with the tofu, crumbling the tofu with your hands. Mix in the ginger, scallions, cornstarch, and salt. Knead the mixture until well mixed.

3 On a cutting board, lay out several wrappers. In the center of each, place 1 level tablespoon of filling. Using a pastry brush, dampen one half of the edge of a wrapper with cool water and pull the 2 sides up over the filling. Press to seal. Pinch the edge into a series of pleats and flatten the bottom of the dumpling. Then place the dumpling on the steamer tray or plate. Continue until all the dumplings are formed.

4 Steam the dumplings over boiling water for 8 minutes. Serve hot with the dipping sauce.

5 **To make the sauce:** In a spice grinder or mortar, finely crush the pine nuts. Add the soy sauce, oil, sugar, and garlic and stir. Serve in bowls for dipping.

MUSHROOM PÂTÉ DE CAMPAGNE

with COGNAC *and* PISTACHIOS

MAKES 1 CUP PÂTÉ / SERVES 6

Mushrooms, cognac, pecans, and chunks of pistachio make this dense pâté hearty and beautiful. Try it on crackers and toast, or in the Bành Mi Sandwich with Pickled Daikon and Carrots, page 114.

INGREDIENTS

2 TABLESPOONS OLIVE OIL

½ CUP CHOPPED SHALLOTS

12 OUNCES PORTOBELLO MUSHROOMS,
chopped

2 CLOVES GARLIC,
sliced

1 TABLESPOON CHOPPED FRESH THYME

1 TEASPOON FRESHLY CRACKED BLACK PEPPER

2 TABLESPOONS COGNAC

½ CUP PECANS,
toasted

½ TEASPOON SALT

¼ CUP HALVED PISTACHIOS,
toasted

1 Heat the olive oil in a large skillet over high heat. Add the shallots, mushrooms, garlic, thyme, and black pepper. Lower the heat to medium high and sauté until the mushrooms are dark and reduced and the pan is dry. Add the cognac and boil until the pan is dry, cooking off the alcohol.

2 Purée the pecans in the food processor until finely ground. Add the mushroom mixture and purée. Season with the salt and stir in the pistachios. Pack into an oiled ramekin or mini–bread pan and chill. Unmold onto a plate to serve.

LEMON-PARMESAN ASPARAGUS SPEARS

in PHYLLO

MAKES 16 SPEARS

Finger food with a springtime theme, these crispy spears will make a veggie lover out of anyone. Aim for the fattest spears you can find for this dish. For dipping, the Mint Aioli from the French Lentil Croquettes recipe on page 22 would take this over the top.

INGREDIENTS

OLIVE OIL SPRAY

2 PIECES PHYLLO DOUGH,
thawed overnight in the refrigerator

4 TABLESPOONS FINELY
SHREDDED PARMESAN CHEESE

1 TABLESPOON LEMON ZEST

16 ASPARAGUS SPEARS,
bottoms trimmed

1 Oil a sheet pan and set aside. Place the phyllo on a counter and cover with plastic wrap, then cover that with a barely damp towel, making sure the phyllo is not exposed to air. Mix the cheese and lemon zest together in a small bowl.

....

2 Spritz each sheet of phyllo with oil, then sprinkle half of each with 2 tablespoons of the cheese mixture. Fold each sheet in half and cut it into eight 4-inch-wide pieces. Place each asparagus spear diagonally across each piece of phyllo with the tip pointing to the lower left-hand corner, and fold that corner over the tip. Roll the lower right corner over the spear, and keep rolling to wrap completely. Place seam-side down on the prepared sheet pan. You can tightly wrap the pan and chill for up to 24 hours before baking.

....

3 Bake at 400°F until crisp and golden, about 20 minutes. Serve warm.

PHYLLO MOCK DUCK AND BROCCOLI EGG ROLLS

with PLUM SAUCE

MAKES 10 EGG ROLLS

Everyone loves fried treats, but nobody really wants to deep-fry at home. These crispy bites are baked, so you skip the vat of oil without sacrificing the crunch you crave. Chewy mock duck and crunchy broccoli are crowd-pleasing and substantial. Vegans will be happy to have an "egg roll" with no eggs in the wrapper, and a fab sauce, to boot!

INGREDIENTS

2 TEASPOONS HOISIN SAUCE

1 TEASPOON ORANGE JUICE

1 TEASPOON SOY SAUCE

1 TEASPOON CORNSTARCH

1 TEASPOON SUGAR

VEGETABLE OIL SPRAY

½ CUP GRATED CARROTS

1½ CUPS CHOPPED CHINESE BROCCOLI
or BROCCOLINI,
in ½-inch pieces

2 CLOVES GARLIC

1 TABLESPOON FRESH GINGER

¼ CUP CANNED SLICED WATER CHESTNUTS,
drained and chopped

10 OUNCES MOCK DUCK,
drained and chopped

2 TABLESPOONS FINELY CHOPPED
ROASTED PEANUTS

5 SHEETS PHYLLO DOUGH,
thawed overnight in the refrigerator

4 TABLESPOONS SESAME OIL

PLUM SAUCE

4 LARGE RED FRESNO CHILES,
chopped

4 TABLESPOONS PLUM JELLY

2 TABLESPOONS SOY SAUCE

4 TABLESPOONS VEGETABLE STOCK

2 TABLESPOONS RICE VINEGAR

2 TEASPOONS CORNSTARCH

1 In a small bowl, whisk together the hoisin sauce, orange juice, soy sauce, cornstarch, and sugar. Set aside.

2 Heat a large nonstick or cast-iron skillet on the stove over medium-high heat. Spray with the oil. Add the carrots and broccoli to the pan and cook, stirring, until broccoli is softened, about 3 to 4 minutes. Add the garlic, ginger, water chestnuts, and mock duck. Stir-fry until heated. Whisk in the soy sauce mixture and cook until thick. Remove from the heat and let cool, then stir in the peanuts.

3 Preheat the oven to 400°F. Place the phyllo sheets on the counter, cut in half across the short side, then cover with plastic wrap and a barely damp towel, making sure the phyllo is not exposed to air. Using a pastry brush, lightly brush half of each half-sheet with the sesame oil. Fold each half-sheet in half to make a square, brush them again with oil, and then fold in half again. Spread ¼ cup of filling to form a line across the bottom of a strip, then pull the edges over it and roll up. Get a heavy baking sheet pan for baking the rolls. Brush oil onto a spot on the pan for the roll, then place the roll seam-side down. Brush it with oil to coat lightly. Continue to make 10 rolls.

4 Bake until crispy and golden brown, 20 to 25 minutes. Serve the rolls hot; the phyllo will soften as it cools.

5 To make the plum sauce: Combine the chiles, jelly, soy sauce, stock, vinegar, and cornstarch in a small saucepan. Heat over medium heat, whisking, until the sauce boils. Reduce the heat and cook for 1 minute, then remove from the heat and transfer the sauce to dipping bowls.

PINEAPPLE-TOFU SUMMER ROLLS

with SATAY SAUCE

MAKES 12 SUMMER ROLLS

At a Vietnamese restaurant, the typical spring roll for vegans is filled with just cilantro and rice noodles, if you're lucky. The pineapple, mint, and crisp veggies in this recipe are a welcome and exciting combination in the delicate rice wrappers.

INGREDIENTS

1 SMALL JICAMA

3 SCALLIONS

1 POUND FIRM TOFU,
drained and pressed

3 TABLESPOONS RICE WINE VINEGAR

2 TABLESPOONS BROWN *or* PALM SUGAR

½ TEASPOON SALT

½ TEASPOON FRESHLY CRACKED BLACK PEPPER

4 OUNCES RICE VERMICELLI *or*
VERY FINE ANGEL HAIR PASTA

TWELVE 8-INCH RICE PAPER ROUNDS

½ SMALL PINEAPPLE,
peeled and sliced into ½-inch sticks

2 CUPS FRESH MINT LEAVES,
washed and dried

SATAY SAUCE

1 CUP COCONUT MILK

1 TABLESPOON RED CURRY PASTE

2 TABLESPOONS BROWN *or* PALM SUGAR

½ TEASPOON SALT

1 TABLESPOON FRESH LEMON JUICE

¼ CUP CREAMY PEANUT BUTTER

1 Slice the jicama and scallions into thin matchsticks and keep them in separate piles. Slice the tofu into 12 slices by first cutting it into 3 long slabs, then cutting the stack into 4. Stir together the rice wine vinegar, sugar, salt, and pepper. Set aside.

2 Boil a pot of water for the noodles. Cook the noodles, stirring and testing often, until tender. Drain and rinse with cold water and drain well again. Wrap the noodles in a kitchen towel and gently squeeze to dry thoroughly. Transfer the noodles to a bowl. Stir the reserved vinegar mixture and mix it into the noodles.

3 Set up your work area for assembling the rolls as follows: a lasagna-size pan with an inch of very warm water in it, a clean towel (at least 12 by 20 inches) spread out next to it, a cutting board, a plate, and plastic wrap for the finished rolls.

4 Submerge a rice paper round in the water and gently swish. Once they are pliable but not completely limp (30 to 60 seconds, depending on the temperature of the water), carefully place on the towel, then transfer to the cutting board. On each round, place a strip of tofu, about ¼ cup noodles, and ¹⁄₁₂ of each of the jicama, scallions, pineapple, and mint leaves. Fold in from the sides and roll up. Put on a platter (not touching) and cover with wet paper towels and plastic wrap until time to serve.

5 **To make the sauce:** Whisk the coconut milk and curry paste in a small saucepan and heat until boiling. Whisk in the sugar, salt, lemon juice, and peanut butter. Bring to a simmer until thick, 3 to 5 minutes. Serve at room temperature.

ROASTED PARSNIP AND GRUYÈRE STRUDELS

MAKES 12 APPETIZER-SIZE PASTRIES

Sweet parsnips and nutty Gruyère are a tasty match—and one quite different from the phyllo appetizers you may have had before. The crispy phyllo here is made lighter by the use of olive oil; or, for a richer dish, simply brush the phyllo sheets with butter. You can also make this as one big pie— just layer the sheets on a baking pan, then put the filling down the middle and fold the phyllo over.

INGREDIENTS

2 POUNDS PARSNIPS,
peeled, quartered, and sliced

2 LARGE CARROTS,
peeled, quartered, and sliced

1 CUP CHOPPED ONION

2 TABLESPOONS CHOPPED FRESH THYME

2 TABLESPOONS EXTRA-VIRGIN
OLIVE OIL *or* BUTTER

¼ CUP FRESH CHOPPED PARSLEY

4 OUNCES GRUYÈRE CHEESE,
shredded

1 TEASPOON SALT

½ TEASPOON FRESH CRACKED
BLACK PEPPER

OLIVE OIL SPRAY

6 SHEETS PHYLLO,
thawed overnight in the refrigerator

1 Preheat the oven to 400°F. Place the parsnips and carrots in a large roasting pan. Add the onion, thyme, and olive oil, and toss. Cover with foil and roast for 20 minutes, stir and re-cover and roast for 20 minutes more, then uncover and roast for an additional 10 to 20 minutes until lightly browned. Let cool.

2 Mix the parsley and Gruyère with the parsnip mixture and season with the salt and pepper. Coat a sheet pan with the olive oil spray. Place the phyllo on the counter, cover with plastic wrap, then cover that with a barely damp towel, making sure the phyllo is not exposed to air. Take a sheet of phyllo, cut it in half across the short side, and then spray it with olive oil. Fold the half-sheet in half, making a tall strip. Place ¼ cup of the parsnip mixture on the bottom of the sheet and fold up flag-style, forming a triangle as you pull the lower left corner up to the right edge, and then the lower right corner up to the left, alternating as you go. Place seam-side down on the sheet pan. Repeat with all sheets.

3 Bake uncovered until browned and crisp, about 20 minutes. Serve warm.

SPICY TOFU YAM TEMAKI ZUSHI HAND ROLLS

MAKES 12 HAND ROLLS

Vegetarians at a traditional sushi bar might get bored with plain rice and veggies, all of which are designed as bland sidekicks to slivers of fish. Making white sushi rice with a little quinoa mixed in gives the tender rice a nutty note, adding to the spicy flavors in the roll. Japanese chili spices and mâche add kick, and wasabi and ginger finish it perfectly.

INGREDIENTS

¾ CUP SUSHI RICE,
washed and drained

¼ CUP QUINOA,
washed and drained

1 TABLESPOON RICE VINEGAR

1 TEASPOON SUGAR

6 OUNCES FIRM TOFU,
drained and pressed

2 TABLESPOONS CORNSTARCH

¾ TEASPOON SALT

1 LARGE EGG

2 TABLESPOONS NANAMI *or*
SHICHIMI TOGARASHI,
*(Japanese chili, sesame,
and orange zest mixture)*

VEGETABLE OIL SPRAY

½ MEDIUM GARNET YAM
(5 ounces)

1 TEASPOON HOT SESAME OIL

6 SHEETS NORI,
cut in half

2 TEASPOONS WASABI

12 SPRIGS MÂCHE

12 PINCHES OF SUNFLOWER
SPROUTS *or* CHIVES

PICKLED GINGER

SHOYU

1 Put the rice and quinoa in a 1-quart saucepan with a lid and add 1½ cups water. Bring to a boil, then reduce heat to low and simmer for 15 minutes. Let stand, covered, off the heat for 5 minutes, then spread the grain on a plate and cover with a wet towel. Heat the vinegar and sugar and fold it into the grain mixture with a rice paddle. Set aside.

2 Preheat the oven to 400°F. Slice the tofu into ⅓-inch-wide strips across the short side of the block. On a small plate, mix the cornstarch and ½ teaspoon salt. Crack the egg into a small bowl and whisk. On another small plate, spread the Nanami. Coat a sheet pan with vegetable oil. Dip each tofu slice in the cornstarch mixture to coat, then dip it in the egg and roll it in Nanami to coat. Place on the prepared pan. Bake for 25 minutes, then let cool.

3 Cut the yam into slices the same thickness as the tofu. Coat a sheet pan with the vegtable spray, then toss the yam slices with the hot sesame oil on the pan and sprinkle with ¼ teaspoon salt. Bake at 400°F for 25 minutes, stirring halfway. Let cool.

4 Place cool water with a shot of rice vinegar in a bowl. On each nori sheet, place ¼ cup of the grain mixture on the left half. With wet fingers, pat the grain to cover a square area on the left half of the nori. The corner of the square of rice that is closest to the center is the point of the cone. From that corner to the upper left corner, spread a small dab of wasabi and cover with a sprig of mâche. Along the line of wasabi, place a slice of tofu, a yam strip, and a few sprouts, their leaf ends hanging out over the corner a bit. Roll the nori around the filling, keeping the point of the cone closed. Dab some vinegar water on the exposed nori, and press to seal. Serve with pickled ginger and shoyu for dipping.

SRI LANKAN TEMPEH SKEWERS

with HOT CASHEW SAMBAL

SERVES 4

Tempeh has a great texture and nutty flavor, but it can soak up oil like a sponge. Traditional recipes for tempeh deep-fry it, but not so here. This recipe steams moisture into it, marinates it, and then bakes it for a delicious result.

INGREDIENTS

HOT CASHEW SAMBAL

3 LARGE SERRANO PEPPERS,
stemmed and seeded

½ CUP DRY-ROASTED UNSALTED CASHEWS

1 TABLESPOON PALM SUGAR

3 TABLESPOONS SOY SAUCE

2 TABLESPOONS LIME JUICE

2 TABLESPOONS TAMARIND PULP

1 POUND TEMPEH,
cut into 2-inch pieces

2 TABLESPOONS CHOPPED FRESH GINGER

6 CLOVES GARLIC,
crushed

2 TEASPOONS GROUND CORIANDER

½ TEASPOON TURMERIC

¼ TEASPOON SALT

¼ CUP SOY SAUCE

1 WHOLE RED ONION,
cut into 1-inch chunks

VEGETABLE OIL SPRAY

8 MEDIUM WOODEN SKEWERS,
soaked for 2 hours in cold water

1 **To make the sambal:** Grind the serranos in a food processor or coffee grinder. Add the cashews and process until very finely minced. Add sugar, soy sauce, lime juice, and tamarind pulp, and purée.

2 Steam the tempeh for 5 minutes—don't skip this step or the tempeh will be dry. In a food processor or coffee grinder, make a paste of the ginger, garlic, coriander, turmeric, salt, and soy sauce. Rub the tempeh with the paste, then let it marinate for at least 2 hours.

3 Preheat the oven to 425°F. Heat a heavy baking sheet for 5 minutes. Carefully skewer the tempeh and onion, supporting the cubes with your fingers on either side as you push the skewer through. Remove the baking sheet from the oven, coat with the vegtable oil spray, and put the skewers on the sheet. Spray again and put the sheet back in the oven for 10 minutes. Flip the skewers and bake until brown, about 5 minutes. Serve hot with the sambal.

THAI RED CURRY DEVILED EGGS

SERVES 6

Deviled eggs may seem like old-fashioned picnic fare, but given a fresh take, they will
be the hit of the party. With flavors that echo those of ever-popular Thai food, these are just
a bit spicy. The coconut cream in this recipe is the solid that forms at the top of the can.
Just scoop out the 2 tablespoons called for here and then use the rest for other dishes.

INGREDIENTS

6 LARGE EGGS

¼ CUP MAYONNAISE

2 TABLESPOONS COCONUT CREAM

1½ TEASPOONS RED CURRY PASTE
(Thai Kitchen Curry Paste is a good brand,
with no hidden shrimp)

1 TABLESPOON LIME ZEST

½ TEASPOON SALT

2 TEASPOONS GRATED FRESH GINGER

¼ CUP MINCED SCALLION

¼ CUP CANNED WATER CHESTNUTS,
minced

1 RED CHILE,
cut into strips

1 Place the eggs in a medium saucepan and cover with cold water. Put over high heat and bring to a full, rolling boil. Cover, remove from the heat, and let stand for 15 minutes. Drain, then rinse with cold water and chill in the refrigerator for at least 2 hours or overnight. Placing the eggs on their sides while chilling will help center the yolks.

2 Peel the eggs and cut each in half lengthwise. Scoop out the yolks into a medium bowl. Mash the yolks thoroughly, then stir in the mayonnaise, coconut cream, curry paste, lime zest, and salt. Add the ginger, scallions, and water chestnuts and mix well. Transfer the mixture to a quart-size plastic bag, then cut off a corner of the bag to make a ½-inch hole. Squeeze the bag to fill each egg half with a generous mound of the mixture. Garnish each with a strip of red chile. Chill in the refrigerator until time to serve.

SPANISH SPINACH, ALMOND, AND EGG EMPANADITAS

MAKES 16 EMPANADITAS

Little handheld pastries like these are irresistible as tapas snacks or a vegetarian entrée.
A side of Manchego cheese and olives, or a Spanish bean salad, would complete the meal.

INGREDIENTS

2½ CUPS UNBLEACHED FLOUR

½ CUP MASA CORN FLOUR

½ TEASPOON SALT

1 TEASPOON BAKING POWDER

4 TABLESPOONS UNSALTED BUTTER,
chilled

¼ CUP EXTRA-VIRGIN OLIVE OIL

1 LARGE EGG

½ CUP MILK

FILLING

1½ POUNDS SPINACH,
washed and stemmed

2 TABLESPOONS
EXTRA-VIRGIN OLIVE OIL

4 CLOVES GARLIC,
minced

1 LARGE TOMATO,
chopped and drained

4 LARGE EGGS,
boiled, peeled, and chopped

½ CUP SLIVERED ALMONDS,
*toasted (for a treat,
chop Marcona almonds)*

½ TEASPOON SALT

1 LARGE EGG YOLK

1 TABLESPOON MILK

1 In a large bowl, mix both flours, the salt, and baking powder. Grate in the butter. Sprinkle in the oil and stir lightly to swirl it in. Combine the egg and milk and stir into the dry ingredients. Knead gently until a dough is formed. Divide the dough into 16 pieces. Cover and let rest for 30 minutes. Preheat the oven to 400°F. Line two baking sheets with parchment paper.

2 **To make the filling:** In a large pot over high heat boil an inch of water and add the spinach. Turn it continuously until the leaves are wilted and bright green, then drain. Squeeze the water from the spinach thoroughly, then wrap the spinach in a towel to wring out further. Chop finely.

3 In a large sauté pan over high heat, heat the olive oil, then sauté the garlic briefly. When the pan is dry, turn off the heat and add the tomato. Stir in the spinach, chopped eggs, almonds, and salt. Stir to mix, remove from the heat, and then let cool.

4 Roll out each portion of dough, then place about 3 tablespoons of the filling on each. Fold the dough over and seal, using a fork or braiding the edge. Place on the prepared baking sheet. Just before baking, brush each with the egg yolk thinned with milk. Bake until lightly golden, about 20 minutes. Serve warm.

TIBETAN POTATO-CHEESE MOMOS

MAKES 20 MOMOS / SERVES 10

Tibetan food is traditionally very plain, with almost no vegetables. These momos are filled with comforting potatoes and cabbage and a cheese that attempts to replace the yak cheese used in Tibet. A fiery sauce with tingly Szechuan peppercorns is a great accent to the fluffy buns.

INGREDIENTS

3 CUPS UNBLEACHED FLOUR

½ CUP WHEAT GERM

1 TEASPOON QUICK-RISE YEAST

1¼ CUPS MILK *or* SOY MILK

2 TABLESPOONS SUGAR
or AGAVE SYRUP

½ POUND YUKON GOLD POTATOES

2 TABLESPOONS BUTTER *or* OIL

2 CUPS CHOPPED ONION

2 CUPS CHOPPED CABBAGE

6 OUNCES DRY JACK *or* OTHER AGED CHEESE,
shredded

½ CUP CILANTRO

½ TEASPOON PAPRIKA

½ TEASPOON SALT

TWENTY 2-INCH PARCHMENT PAPER SQUARES

SAUCE

2 TEASPOONS SZECHUAN PEPPERCORNS,
coarsely chopped

2 TEASPOONS RED PEPPER FLAKES

½ TEASPOON SALT

1 CUP CILANTRO LEAVES,
stems removed

2 CLOVES GARLIC

1 CUP FIRE-ROASTED TOMATO PURÉE

1 In a stand mixer or large bowl, combine the flour, wheat germ, and yeast. In a small pot, heat the milk and sugar to 100°F (no hotter or you will kill the yeast). Mix the warm milk into the flour mixture and knead until smooth. Cover with plastic wrap and let rise for 1 hour.

2 In a medium pot, boil the potatoes whole, then drain and mash. Let cool. Heat the butter in a large pan over medium heat. Add the onion and cabbage and sauté until the cabbage is golden, about 5 minutes. Let cool.

3 Mix together the potatoes, onions and cabbage, cheese, cilantro, paprika, and salt.

4 Form the dough into a cylinder and cut it into 20 equal disks. Form each into a ball, then pat and stretch around the edges to make each ball about 3 inches across and thick in the middle. Scoop 2 tablespoons of filling into the center of one ball and pull up the edges, pinching them to seal. Place each bun seam-side down on a parchment square and transfer to a steaming rack or plate. Cover loosely. Continue filling momos until they are all formed. Let the momos rise for 30 to 60 minutes.

5 Put water in the bottom of a large pan or steamer, and bring to a boil. Reduce to a simmer and put the momos over the steam and put on the lid. Steam until the dough is cooked through, about 10 minutes. Serve hot with the sauce.

6 **To make sauce:** Dry-toast the Szechuan peppercorns and red pepper flakes in a small pan over medium-high heat. Transfer to a spice grinder, add the salt, and grind. Add the cilantro and garlic and grind. Transfer to a small bowl and stir in the tomato pureé.

WILD-MUSHROOM-SOUFFLÉ-STUFFED PORTOBELLO MUSHROOMS

MAKES 4 STUFFED MUSHROOMS / SERVES 4

In this showy dish, portobello caps cradle a tasty soufflé. The trick is finding the biggest mushrooms with the best rims, so that you can fit a serving of soufflé in them. For a faster meal, you can make the mushroom base, up to the point of adding the egg yolks, and chill it until it's time to assemble. Just gently reheat it to room temperature, then add the yolk.

INGREDIENTS

4 LARGE PORTOBELLO MUSHROOMS,
stems and gills removed

2 TEASPOONS UNSALTED BUTTER

¼ CUP FINELY CHOPPED SHALLOTS

4 OUNCES CREMINI *or* BABY BELLA MUSHROOMS,
stems removed, minced

2 TEASPOONS UNBLEACHED FLOUR

½ CUP MILK

1½ OUNCES GRUYÈRE CHEESE,
finely shredded

¼ TEASPOON TARRAGON

½ TEASPOON SALT

¼ TEASPOON FRESHLY GROUND PEPPER

1 LARGE EGG YOLK

3 LARGE EGG WHITES

⅛ TEASPOON LEMON JUICE

VEGETABLE OIL SPRAY

1 Salt the insides of the portobellos generously, then place them cut-side down on paper towels to drain on a sheet pan. Chill in the refrigerator. Preheat the oven to 425°F and position a rack in the lower third of the oven.

2 In a 2-quart saucepan over medium heat, melt the butter and sauté the shallots. Reduce the heat if they begin to brown. Add the cremini to the shallots in the pan. Turn up the heat and sauté, stirring continuously, until the mushrooms are shrunken and soft, about 3 minutes. Sprinkle the flour over the mushrooms and stir to incorporate. Remove the pan from the heat and slowly stir in the milk. When all of the milk has been added and mixed, put the pan back over medium heat and cook, stirring continuously. When the mixture comes to a simmer, stir for 1 minute more, then remove from the heat. Stir in the cheese and transfer the mixture to a large bowl. Let cool for 5 minutes, then stir in the tarragon, the salt, and the pepper. The mixture can be made up to this point and chilled for assembly later. When ready to finish, stir in the egg yolk.

3 Using an electric mixer, beat the egg whites with lemon juice until they form firm peaks. Fold one-quarter of the beaten whites into the mushroom mixture. Fold in the rest of the whites. Take the mushroom caps out of the fridge and thoroughly dry them inside. Coat a sheet pan with vegetable oil spray. Return the mushrooms to the pan. Divide the egg mixture among the 4 mushroom caps. (If you have extra filling, bake it in a small ramekin.) Put the pan on the bottom rack in the oven, close the door, and reduce the heat to 350°F. Bake until puffed and well-browned and a toothpick inserted into the center of a soufflé comes out with no wet eggs sticking to it, 30 to 40 minutes.

CHAPTER 2
SALADS

A SALAD CAN BE JUST ABOUT ANYTHING, AS LONG AS IT HAS A DRESSING ON IT. Crisp greens, tender beans, crunchy nuts, chewy grains, and even fruit make appearances in salads, and the more the merrier. Vegetarians are often suspected of eating nothing but salad, but, oh, the salads vegetarians eat. Take a global tour of cool foods, punched up with proteins and dressed to (not) kill. What could be better on a hot summer day than a one-dish meal, filled with crunch and color? Or a hearty winter salad, all comfort and greenery for the dark months? All these salads are way more substantial than iceberg lettuce, and the dressings put the bottled stuff to shame. Bring a Big Salad to a dinner party, and people will be drawn to the colors like bees to the flower. Tempting people to eat their veggies is an act of love.

BIG SALAD

with CARAMELIZED PUMPKINSEEDS, PEARS, and POMEGRANATE

SERVES 6

This great wintertime salad is best prepared with pomegranates, which appear only around the holidays. Tender pears and pumpkinseeds round out this seasonal delight. Vegans can leave out the cheese and enjoy the crunchy spiced seeds instead.

INGREDIENTS

1 TEASPOON EXTRA-VIRGIN OLIVE OIL

1 CUP RAW PUMPKINSEEDS

2 TABLESPOONS BROWN SUGAR

½ TEASPOON CHILI POWDER

¼ TEASPOON CUMIN

¼ TEASPOON CINNAMON

1½ TEASPOONS SALT

1 LARGE CLOVE GARLIC,
peeled

2 TABLESPOONS FRESH MINT
(optional)

2 TABLESPOONS POMEGRANATE
JUICE CONCENTRATE

1 TABLESPOON LEMON JUICE

1 TEASPOON HONEY

¼ CUP PUMPKINSEED or OLIVE OIL

1 SMALL POMEGRANATE

1 LARGE HEAD ROMAINE LETTUCE,
washed and dried

2 SMALL SHALLOTS,
thinly sliced

2 LARGE BOSC PEARS,
sliced

4 OUNCES PECORINO CHEESE,
sliced

1 Heat the 1 teaspoon olive oil over high heat for 1 minute in a medium nonstick skillet. Add the pumpkinseeds and toss in the pan until the seeds are popping and browning, about 3 minutes. Remove the pan from the heat and add the brown sugar, tossing continuously until the seeds are coated with melted sugar (careful—it will burn easily). Quickly mix in chili powder, cumin, cinnamon, and 1 teaspoon of the salt, then spread the mixture on a plate. Let cool completely and store in an airtight container for up to 1 week until ready to use.

2 In food processor, mince the garlic and mint (if using). Add the pomegranate juice concentrate, lemon juice, honey, and the remaining ½ teaspoon salt and pulse to mix. With the machine running, gradually drizzle in ¼ pumpkinseed or olive oil. Set the dressing aside.

3 Cut through the skin of the pomegranate from stem to tip, dividing the fruit in quarters. Hold it over a bowl and pull apart the sections, then tear apart the pieces, gently freeing the seeds. Slice across the Romaine leaves into ½-inch-wide strips. Arrange the greens on plates or in a large bowl. Top with the shallots, pears, and cheese. Drizzle the dressing over the salad and top with the pomegranate seeds and pumpkinseeds. Serve immediately.

FRENCH APPLE-PEAR SALAD

SERVES 4

You will love the spears of delicate pear and tangy apple dressed with simple nut oil and lemon. Toasted walnuts add weight and depth. And if you want to make a meal of it, add cheese for a complement.

INGREDIENTS

2 LARGE HONEYCRISP or FUJI APPLES

2 LARGE BOSC or 6 LUSCIOUS PEARS

2 RIBS CELERY,
chopped

2 TABLESPOONS LEMON JUICE

½ TEASPOON VANILLA EXTRACT

¼ CUP WALNUT OIL

1 PINCH SALT

3 TABLESPOONS COARSELY
CHOPPED FRESH TARRAGON

½ CUP WALNUTS,
toasted

TARRAGON SPRIGS

BRIE OR BLUE CHEESE
(optional)

1 Slice the apples and pears in half and cut out the cores. Slice them into long spears and place them in a medium bowl with the celery.

2 In a small bowl or cup, whisk the lemon juice and vanilla. Whisk in the walnut oil and salt.

3 Pour the dressing over the fruit. Add the chopped tarragon and toss to coat. Serve on individual plates topped with walnuts and garnished with tarragon sprigs and a wedge of Brie, if desired.

GOLDEN KAMUT SALAD PRIMAVERA

SERVES 6

Kamut is a variety of wheat that produces longer, plumper grains than the typical red winter wheat. It is wonderful for salads because of its size, crunch, and buttery taste. If you can't find it, though, use wheat berries. The dressing relies on chèvre and kefir for creamy richness, with just a touch of oil for flavor.

INGREDIENTS

1 CUP KAMUT,
rinsed

1 CLOVE GARLIC

1½ OUNCES CHÈVRE,
keep at room temperature

1 TABLESPOON LEMON JUICE

2 TABLESPOONS
EXTRA-VIRGIN OLIVE OIL

½ CUP PLAIN LOW-FAT KEFIR *or* YOGURT

4 OUNCES SNAP PEAS,
trimmed

4 OUNCES FRENCH BEANS,
trimmed

1 BUNCH ASPARAGUS,
cut into 2-inch pieces

4 MEDIUM BABY CARROTS,
quartered lengthwise

½ CUP WATERCRESS,
washed and dried

6 LARGE CHERRY TOMATOES,
quartered

1 Put the kamut in a small saucepan with plenty of water and boil until tender, about 45 minutes. Drain and let cool.

2 In a food processor, mince the garlic. Add the chèvre and purée, scraping down the sides. Add the lemon juice and process until smooth. With the machine running, pour in the olive oil, then add the kefir. Set aside.

3 Put the peas, French beans, asparagus, and carrots in a steamer and steam until crisp-tender, about 3 minutes. Transfer the vegetables to a kitchen towel and pat dry.

4 Pour half of the dressing over the kamut and toss with the watercress, then spread the mixture on a platter or individual plates. Toss the steamed vegetables and tomatoes with the remaining dressing and spread them over the grain before serving.

LIGHT TUSCAN BEAN AND KALE SALAD

with GORGONZOLA BRUSCHETTA

SERVES 4

Light, flavorful balsamic dressing is made low-fat by using stock as a base in this recipe.
Just a touch of flavorful olive oil and crunchy kale give these creamy beans all the flavor of Tuscany.

INGREDIENTS

¾ CUP VEGETABLE STOCK

2 TEASPOONS CORNSTARCH

1 TEASPOON BROWN SUGAR

1 TEASPOON SALT

2 TABLESPOONS CHOPPED
FRESH ROSEMARY

4 CLOVES GARLIC,
chopped

¼ CUP BALSAMIC VINEGAR

½ TEASPOON RED PEPPER FLAKES

3 TABLESPOONS EXTRA-VIRGIN OLIVE OIL

1 BUNCH KALE,
stems removed

ONE 15-OUNCE CAN NAVY BEANS

ONE 15-OUNCE CAN KIDNEY BEANS

1 LARGE BEEFSTEAK TOMATO,
diced

GORGONZOLA BRUSCHETTA

16 SLICES WHOLE WHEAT BAGUETTE,
thinly sliced on the diagonal

½ CUP FRESH BASIL

1 TEASPOON EXTRA-VIRGIN OLIVE OIL

1 PINCH KOSHER SALT

¼ CUP (½ OUNCE) CRUMBLED
GORGONZOLA CHEESE

1 Put a large pot of water on to boil. In a small saucepan, combine the stock, cornstarch, sugar, salt, rosemary, and garlic. Stirring continuously, bring to a boil. Then reduce the heat and simmer gently until thickened. Add the vinegar, red pepper flakes, and oil. Simmer briefly, then remove from the heat.

2 Coarsely chop the kale, then drop it into the boiling water. After the water returns to a boil, cook for 2 minutes. Drain thoroughly and then wring out the water. Rinse and drain the navy and kidney beans, then place them on a towel and gently roll them up to let them dry thoroughly. Put the beans in a bowl and gently toss with the kale and dressing. To serve, portion 1 cup of the bean mixture onto each plate, top with the diced tomato, and arrange 4 bruschetta slices around the edges.

3 **To make bruschetta:** Preheat the broiler and place the baguette slices on a sheet pan. Chop the basil finely and mix it with the olive oil and salt in a small bowl. On each slice of bread, portion the basil mixture and gorgonzola on top. Broil until the cheese has melted and browned, about 1 minute (watch carefully to ensure the bruschetta does not burn).

MÂCHE, BLOOD ORANGE, AND PISTACHIO SALAD

SERVES 4

This salad makes use of the dramatic red blood orange in both the salad and the dressing.
It tastes wonderful with orange oranges, too, which are sweeter, so be prepared to add a little
more vinegar if you go this route. For a main course salad, add some Kasseri or feta cheese.

INGREDIENTS

½ CUP PISTACHIO

1 CLOVE GARLIC,
peeled

¼ CUP BLOOD ORANGE JUICE
(about 1 orange), with zest

1/4 TEASPOON SALT

1 TABLESPOON RED WINE VINEGAR

1 TABLESPOON HONEY

½ CUP EXTRA-VIRGIN OLIVE OIL

4 OUNCES MÂCHE,
washed and dried

1 CUP SHREDDED CARROTS

2 LARGE BLOOD ORANGES,
peeled and sliced

1 Toast the pistachios in a 300°F oven until lightly golden, about 10 minutes. Coarsely chop and reserve half of the nuts. Place the other half in a blender or food processor and purée with the garlic, scraping down to make a paste. Add the blood orange juice and zest, salt, vinegar, and honey and purée to mix well. With the machine running, pour in the oil to make an emulsified dressing. Taste a drop of dressing on a mâche leaf—if the oranges were not acidic enough, add a few more drops of vinegar for tartness.

....

2 On a platter, distribute the mâche. Top with the carrot shreds and orange slices. Pour the dressing over the salad and garnish with the reserved pistachios. Serve immediately.

NONYA SALAD

with EGGS *and* TAMARIND DRESSING

SERVES 6

This makes a huge salad, fresh and full of vibrant flavors and textures, and it's quite low in fat. Krupuk are sold in Asian markets as flat, hard disks that puff up to crispy chips when deep-fried. They are made from pounded nuts and rice and are sometimes seafood-flavored, so beware. They are part of Indonesian cuisine and absolutely addictive.

INGREDIENTS

8 LARGE EGGS

2 RED CHILES,
minced

4 CLOVES GARLIC,
crushed

1 TABLESPOON TAMARIND PULP

¼ CUP PALM SUGAR

1 TEASPOON LIME ZEST

¼ CUP LIME JUICE

1 TABLESPOON SOY SAUCE

1 TEASPOON DARK SESAME OIL

1 SMALL CARROT,
shredded

1 SMALL DAIKON,
shredded

1 MEDIUM MANGO,
peeled and sliced

1 MEDIUM CUCUMBER,
peeled and sliced

2 TOMATOES,
cut into wedges

1 CUP CILANTRO LEAVES,
stems removed

1 HEAD BIBB LETTUCE,
washed and dried

2 TABLESPOONS PREPARED FRIED SHALLOT

TOASTED CASHEWS
(optional)

FRIED KRUPUK
(optional)

1 Place the eggs in a 2-quart pot over high heat with enough cold water to cover by 1 inch. Bring to a full boil, watching carefully. As soon as it boils, cover the pan, remove from the heat, and let stand for 15 minutes. Drain eggs and run cold water over them until cooled. Chill, then peel. Cut each egg in half from tip to end and set aside.

....

2 Whisk the chiles, garlic, tamarind, palm sugar, lime zest and juice, soy sauce, and sesame oil to make a dressing.

....

3 Compose the carrot, daikon, mango, cucumber, tomatoes, and cilantro on a bed of Bibb lettuce. Top with the halved eggs and drizzle with the dressing. Garnish with fried shallots and toasted cashews and the fried krupuk, if desired.

NEW POTATO–GARBANZO SALAD
with AVOCADO DRESSING *and* SMOKED ALMONDS

SERVES 4

Potato salad can be an exciting dish, especially with this creamy avocado-buttermilk dressing and crunchy smoked almonds. Avocados and almonds provide some of the healthiest fats around, and using them this way stretches their fabulousness through a whole meal.

INGREDIENTS

12 OUNCES NEW POTATOES

1 CUP COOKED GARBANZO BEANS,
drained

¼ CUP SLICED RED ONION

1 CLOVE GARLIC,
peeled

1 LARGE JALAPEÑO,
seeded

1 SMALL AVOCADO,
pitted

5 TABLESPOONS BUTTERMILK

1 TEASPOON LIME JUICE

¾ TEASPOON SALT

12 SMALL ROMAINE LETTUCE LEAVES,
washed and dried

½ CUP CILANTRO LEAVES,
stems removed

½ CUP SMOKED ALMONDS,
coarsely chopped

1 Boil the new potatoes whole until tender when pierced with a paring knife. Drain and chill. When cooled, halve the potatoes into a large bowl and add the beans and red onion.

2 In a food processor, mince the garlic and jalapeño. Scrape down, add the avocado, and purée. Add the buttermilk, lime juice, and salt and process until smooth.

3 Pour the dressing over the potato mixture and toss to coat. Serve on a bed of lettuce leaves on one large plate or on individual plates. Top with the cilantro and almonds before serving.

ROASTED BABY BEET AND TOFU SALAD

with WASABI DRESSING

SERVES 4

A bunch of early summer beets inspired this recipe, a dramatic dish of scarlet tofu colored by beet juices. Japanese flavors complement the earthy beets as well as the tofu. Add the dressing just before serving or it will slowly turn pink as well.

INGREDIENTS

1 TABLESPOON EXTRA-VIRGIN OLIVE OIL

12 OUNCES FIRM TOFU,
drained and pressed

6 SMALL BEETS WITH GREENS,
washed

½ TEASPOON HOT SESAME OIL

1 TABLESPOON CHOPPED FRESH GINGER

1 TABLESPOON PONZU SAUCE

¼ CUP MAYONNAISE

¼ CUP PLAIN YOGURT

2 TABLESPOONS WASABI PASTE

2 SMALL SCALLIONS,
sliced diagonally

1 Preheat the oven to 400°F. Spread the olive oil in a large roasting pan. Cut the tofu into ½-inch cubes. Remove the greens from the beets and set aside. Peel and cube the beets approximately the same size as the tofu cubes. Add the hot sesame oil and ginger and toss gently. Roast uncovered for 20 minutes, then use a metal spatula to turn the beets and tofu. Bake for 20 minutes more. Let cool.

....

2 Place the reserved beet greens in a large pot with a lid over high heat. The greens will be steaming after a couple of minutes. Use tongs to turn them when they go limp. Once they are softened, add the ponzu and stir until it evaporates. Transfer the greens to a plate and let cool.

....

3 In a small bowl, whisk the mayonnaise, yogurt, and wasabi. Arrange the beet greens on the plate, then arrange the tofu mixture on top of them. Drizzle the wasabi dressing over the greens and tofu, sprinkle the scallions on top, and serve.

ROASTED GRAPES AND GOLDEN BEETS ON ARUGULA

with PISTACHIO CHÈVRE

SERVES 6

This is a great winter salad, with plump red roasted grapes and sunny beets, topped with green pistachio–studded chèvre.

INGREDIENTS

2 CUPS RED GRAPES,
stems removed

OLIVE OIL FOR ROASTING

8 SMALL GOLDEN BEETS

1 CUP APPLE JUICE

¼ LARGE GRANNY SMITH APPLE,
finely chopped

1 TABLESPOON JULIENNED FRESH GINGER

1 TABLESPOON FRESH LEMON JUICE

2 TABLESPOONS EXTRA-VIRGIN OLIVE OIL

SALT

FRESHLY CRACKED BLACK PEPPER

SUGAR *or* MAPLE SYRUP,
to taste (optional)

½ CUP PISTACHIOS,
chopped

½ TEASPOON MINCED FRESH THYME,
plus THYME SPRIGS *for garnish*

8 OUNCES CHÈVRE,
chilled

5 OUNCES ARUGULA,
washed and dried

1 Preheat the oven to 300°F. Toss the grapes with a drizzle of olive oil in a small baking pan. Peel the beets and put them in another baking pan with a drizzle of olive oil, toss, cover with foil, and put them in the oven with the grapes. After 20 minutes, remove the grapes from the oven, then raise the heat to 400°F and roast the beets until tender, about 20 minutes more. Let the beets cool and then halve vertically.

2 In a small saucepan, bring the apple juice, apple, and ginger to a simmer. Cook until it's reduced to a syrup. Let cool. Then whisk in the lemon juice and olive oil and season with salt and pepper. If too sour, add a pinch of sugar.

3 Mix the pistachios and thyme on a plate. Cut the log of cheese into 6 slices, then dip the slices in the pistachio mixture. Let come to room temperature.

4 Spread the arugula on a platter or individual salad plates. Arrange the beets around the edges and pile the grapes in the center. Drizzle the dressing over the salads and place the cheese on top. Garnish salads with thyme sprigs. Serve immediately.

SMOKY HERB SALAD

with TOMATO VINAIGRETTE

SERVES 4

Smoky flavors add depth and umami to this salad, as well as the taste of the
summer grill. If you'd like to try something other than the spring herb salad mix,
use mesclun or other greens and throw in some fresh basil and arugula.

INGREDIENTS

2 SUN-DRIED TOMATOES

1 CLOVE GARLIC

2 TABLESPOONS SHERRY VINEGAR

1 PINCH SMOKED PAPRIKA *or*
CHIPOTLE POWDER,
or to taste

1 TEASPOON HONEY

⅛ TEASPOON SALT

¼ CUP NUT OIL *or* OLIVE OIL

5 OUNCES MIXED GREENS
AND FRESH HERBS,
washed and dried

1 LARGE HEIRLOOM TOMATO,
cut into wedges

4 OUNCES MUSHROOMS,
sliced

2 OUNCES SMOKED MOZZARELLA *or*
OTHER SMOKED CHEESE,
slivered

½ CUP SMOKED ALMONDS

FRESHLY CRACKED BLACK PEPPER

1 Pour boiling water over the sun-dried tomatoes and soak them until
completely soft. Drain the water from the tomatoes, chop, then place them in
a food processor and purée. Add the garlic and pulse to chop. Add the vinegar,
scraping down the sides to get a smooth purée. Add the smoked paprika,
honey, and salt and, with the machine running, drizzle in the oil to make an
emulsified dressing.

2 Layer the greens and herbs, tomato wedges, and mushrooms on a platter.
Sprinkle the mozzarella and almonds on top. Grind pepper over the salad.
Drizzle the dressing over all. Serve immediately.

TOFU CAPRESE SALAD

SERVES 4

A fresh summer tomato is a joy unto itself. Infusing tofu with lemon and olive oil makes a chewy stand-in for cheese in the classic Italian salad. You may just like it better.

INGREDIENTS

1 POUND FIRM TOFU,
drained and pressed

4 TABLESPOONS
EXTRA-VIRGIN OLIVE OIL

4 TABLESPOONS LEMON JUICE

½ TEASPOON PLUS 2 PINCHES SALT

½ TEASPOON FRESHLY
CRACKED BLACK PEPPER

THREE 4- TO 5-INCH RIPE TOMATOES

1 CUP FRESH BASIL,
washed and dried

3 CLOVES GARLIC,
crushed

1 Slice the tofu into ¼-inch-thick slabs. Mix together 2 tablespoons of the olive oil, 2 tablespoons of the lemon juice, the ½ teaspoon salt, and ¼ teaspoon of the pepper. Marinate the tofu in this mixture for at least 1 hour, or overnight.

2 Preheat the oven to 400°F, pour the tofu and marinade into a baking pan, and bake for 20 minutes. Flip the tofu and bake for 10 minutes more. Let cool completely.

3 Core and slice the tomatoes and build a spiral in a low bowl by alternating tomatoes, tofu, and individual basil leaves.

4 In a cup, stir together the remaining 2 tablespoons olive oil, 2 tablespoons lemon juice, the garlic, and the remaining ¼ teaspoon pepper. Drizzle this dressing over the salad, sprinkle with a few pinches of salt, and serve immediately.

TRIO OF SUMMER SUNOMONO SALADS

SERVES 4

This may look like a long recipe, but these light, fresh salads are easy to make. You can make just one, but the combination of the three brings the balance of colors that make up a washoku meal, as described by Elizabeth Andoh in her book *Washoku: Recipes from the Japanese Home Kitchen*. The trio also makes the most of summer goodness with a nutritional boost from sea vegetables.

INGREDIENTS

CORN SALAD

2 EARS SWEET CORN,
kernels cut off

1 CUP FROZEN EDAMAME,
thawed

¼ CUP RICE VINEGAR

2 TABLESPOONS MIRIN

1 TABLESPOON SOY SAUCE

2 TEASPOONS SUGAR

1 TABLESPOON GRATED FRESH GINGER

½ TEASPOON SESAME OIL

¼ TEASPOON SALT

½ CUP SHISO LEAF *or*
FRESH BASIL,
slivered

WAKAME SALAD

1 OUNCE WAKAME

1 MEDIUM CARROT,
finely julienned

3 TABLESPOONS RICE VINEGAR

1 TABLESPOON SUGAR

2 TABLESPOONS SOY SAUCE

2 TEASPOONS GRATED FRESH GINGER

1 LARGE RED CHILE,
chopped

2 TABLESPOONS SESAME SEEDS,
toasted

TOFU SALAD

1 PACKAGE SILKEN TOFU,
drained and pressed

2 LARGE RIPE TOMATOES,
seeded

2 TABLESPOONS UME PLUM VINEGAR

2 TABLESPOONS HONEY

2 TABLESPOONS CHOPPED CHIVES

CORN SALAD

Steam the corn kernels until crisp-tender, about 2 minutes. Dry the corn and edamame in a clean kitchen towel. In a cup, mix vinegar, mirin, soy sauce, sugar, ginger, sesame oil, the salt, and the shiso. Add the corn and edamame and toss.

....

WAKAME SALAD

Soak the wakame in cool water for 30 minutes, then drain and squeeze out excess water. Chop the wakame into 1-inch segments, if necessary. Put the wakame in a medium bowl with the carrots. In a cup, whisk the vinegar, sugar, soy sauce, ginger, and red chiles. Pour this dressing over the wakame. Top with the sesame seeds.

....

TOFU SALAD

Dice the tofu and tomatoes into cubes of the same size and place them in a medium bowl. In a cup, whisk the vinegar, honey, and chives. Pour this dressing over the tofu and tomatoes and gently toss to coat.

....

To serve, give each diner a medium plate and compose ½ cup each of the corn and tofu salads alongside ¼ cup of the wakame salad.

CHAPTER 3
SOUPS

SOUP HAS TO BE THE MOST UNIVERSAL AND ELEMENTAL OF FOODS. Yet, most restaurants serve terrible soup, probably straight out of cans and frozen blocks. The reason they get it all so wrong is that soup takes a little love and care. Making a stock, whether veggie or meat based, is a step that your typical industrial kitchen leaves to manufacturers of powders and pastes, and you can taste it. In these soups, you will employ a full range of natural vegetarian tricks that make hearty, satisfying soups, and, yes, you will use some high-quality, boxed vegetable stocks. I recommend Imagine or Pacific Organic brands, and avoid cans because they give delicate stock an off-taste.

A flavor concept that vegetarians would do well to understand is called "umami," and it is crucial to soup making. The Japanese coined the phrase to describe the fifth taste, which is really the sense of "meatiness" or satisfying mouth-filling qualities that are sought after in their cuisine. This quality is not just a descriptor, but an actual chemical event. When proteins are broken down by fermentation, they break into glutamates and other chemicals that are the source of umami. That gives miso, soy sauce, black bean sauce, and aged cheeses that extra savory quality. These same kinds of chemicals are in mushrooms, tomatoes at peak ripeness, seaweeds, and dried vegetables.

Vegetarian soups that are made with umami-rich ingredients will put the lie to the myth that you need chicken stock to make good soup. Try these recipes, and I'm sure you will agree!

MEXICAN CORN AND QUINOA
with CHIPOTLE BEANS *and* PICKLED ONIONS

SERVES 3

This recipe may appear fussy, but the three quick, simple elements of corn, beans, and onions come together fast and look great on the plate. Their distinct flavors and textures make your bowl of soup much more interesting and build a balanced meal at the same tasty time.

INGREDIENTS

1 TABLESPOON COLD-PRESSED CORN OIL

½ CUP CHOPPED YELLOW ONION

2 LARGE RED FRESNO CHILES,
chopped

1 CLOVE GARLIC,
chopped

¼ CUP QUINOA

1½ CUPS VEGETABLE STOCK

1 TABLESPOON CHOPPED FRESH THYME

2 CUPS CORN KERNELS,
frozen or fresh

1 TEASPOON SALT

¼ CUP CREAM *or* CRÈME FRAÎCHE
(optional)

1 TABLESPOON RED WINE VINEGAR

1 TABLESPOON SUGAR

¼ CUP THINLY SHAVED RED ONION

ONE 15-OUNCE CAN BLACK BEANS,
drained and rinsed

1 TEASPOON CUMIN

¼ TEASPOON CHIPOTLE PEPPER POWDER

½ CUP FIRE-ROASTED DICED TOMATOES

1 In a 2-quart pot, over medium-high heat, heat the oil and sauté the onions for 5 minutes. Add the chiles and garlic, stir for 1 minute, then add the quinoa, vegetable stock, and the thyme. Bring to a boil. Cover and lower the heat and cook for 15 minutes. Add the corn and simmer until cooked. Stir in the ½ teaspoon of salt and the cream (if using).

....

2 In a small bowl, stir the vinegar and sugar, then toss with red onion slices. Let stand.

....

3 In a small saucepan, heat the beans, cumin, chipotle, the remaining ½ teaspoon salt, and the tomatoes, stirring and mashing a few of the beans to thicken the mixture.

....

4 Ladle a cup of the corn soup into a wide bowl, then scoop ½ cup of the black bean mixture into the center. Top with a third of the pickled onions and serve.

AFRICAN GARBANZO, PEANUT, AND KALE SOUP

MAKES 6 CUPS / SERVES 4

Vegetarians love peanut butter, and peanut butter loves them back, with inexpensive, tasty protein that keeps in the pantry. African groundnut stews often contain chicken, but this creamy concoction is pure veg and includes the kale we love to eat.

INGREDIENTS

1 TABLESPOON EXTRA-VIRGIN OLIVE OIL

1 MEDIUM ONION, *chopped*

1 LARGE CARROT, *thinly sliced*

1 CLOVE GARLIC, *minced*

6 TABLESPOONS SMOOTH PEANUT BUTTER

2 CUPS VEGETABLE STOCK

1 TEASPOON PAPRIKA

1 TEASPOON CORIANDER

¼ TEASPOON CAYENNE PEPPER

1 CUP TOMATO PURÉE

ONE 15-OUNCE CAN GARBANZO BEANS, *drained and rinced*

2 CUPS CHOPPED KALE

SALT

FRESHLY CRACKED BLACK PEPPER

1 In a large pot over medium heat, heat the olive oil. Add the onion and carrot and sauté until soft and golden, about 5 minutes. Add the garlic and cook for a few minutes more, stirring.

....

2 In a food processor or by hand, mix the peanut butter and a little of the vegetable stock to make a smooth paste. Set aside. Blend the rest of the vegetable stock into the mixture.

....

3 Add the paprika, coriander, and cayenne to the onion mixture and return to the heat. Cook, stirring, until fragrant, about 1 minute. Add the peanut butter mixture, tomato purée, beans, and kale. Bring the mixture to a simmer. Cook for about 5 minutes until kale is tender and soup is thickened, and season with salt and pepper. Serve hot. Accompany with flatbreads, cooked millet, or brown rice.

EASY SPLIT PEA SOUP

with SPINACH

MAKES ABOUT 7 CUPS / SERVES 6

Split peas cook faster than beans and make a comforting, thick soup. To shave a few minutes from the cooking time, soak the split peas overnight. This warming soup is simple, with peasant-style flavors and lots of bright spinach added at the end. Make a double batch and freeze some.

INGREDIENTS

1 CUP SPLIT PEAS,
sorted and washed

¼ CUP SHORT-GRAIN BROWN RICE

1 LARGE BAY LEAF

4 WHOLE CLOVES GARLIC,
peeled

1 MEDIUM CARROT,
chopped

2 STALKS CELERY,
chopped

2 TABLESPOONS CHOPPED FRESH ROSEMARY

1 SMALL ONION,
chopped

1 CUP CANNED DICED TOMATOES

½ CUP WHITE WINE

½ TEASPOON OREGANO

1 TEASPOON SALT
plus more to taste

1 TEASPOON FRESHLY CRACKED BLACK PEPPER
plus more to taste

5 OUNCES SPINACH LEAVES,
coarsely chopped

1 In a large 6-quart pot over high heat, bring to a boil 8 cups of water, the split peas, brown rice, bay leaf, garlic, carrot, celery, rosemary, and onion. Reduce the heat, cover, and simmer for 1½ hours, stirring occasionally. Add more water if needed.

2 When the split peas are falling apart, add the tomatoes, wine, oregano, the salt and the pepper, and simmer for 10 minutes more. Just before serving, stir in the spinach and simmer just to wilt, then adjust salt and pepper to taste.

FRENCH SPRING VEGETABLE SOUP
with FAVA BEAN PISTOU

MAKES 6 CUPS / SERVES 4

Springtime is a good time to eat fresh, local asparagus. This light, delicious soup is simple and easy, and the whole wheat bread and fava spread make it a filling meal.

INGREDIENTS

FAVA BEAN PISTOU

3 CLOVES GARLIC

1 CUP FRESH BASIL

½ CUP FROZEN
FAVA BEANS *or* EDAMAME,
thawed

2 TABLESPOONS
EXTRA-VIRGIN OLIVE OIL

½ TEASPOON SALT

1 TABLESPOON
EXTRA-VIRGIN OLIVE OIL

1 SMALL TURNIP (6 OUNCES),
cubed

2 LARGE LEEKS,
sliced and washed

1 MEDIUM CARROT,
peeled and chopped

1 TABLESPOON CHOPPED FRESH THYME

1 POUND ASPARAGUS

1 LARGE BAY LEAF

4 CUPS VEGETABLE STOCK

SALT

FRESHLY CRACKED BLACK PEPPER

CRUSTY WHOLEWHEAT BREAD

4 SMALL FRENCH
BREAKFAST RADISHES,
sliced

1 **To make the pistou:** Mince the garlic in a food processor. Add the basil and mince, scraping down the sides a few times. Add the fava beans and process. Scrape down the sides and add the olive oil and the salt. Purée until smooth.

....

2 In a large pot over medium heat, heat the olive oil. Add the turnip, leeks, carrot, and thyme. Sauté until the leeks are softened, stirring often. Cut the tips off the asparagus and set aside. Chop the stems and add them to the pot. Add the bay leaf and vegetable stock, and bring to a simmer. Simmer, covered, for 8 minutes. Add the asparagus tips and cook until softened, about 2 minutes. Taste and season with pepper.

....

3 Serve each bowl of soup with a spoonful of pistou, a hunk of hearty whole wheat bread, the remaining pistou for spreading, and sliced radishes.

INDONESIAN HOT AND SOUR SOUP

with EDAMAME

SERVES 4

The spicy-sour flavors of this soup are made even deeper with the earthy flavor of carrot juice. A little miso gives some umami and saltiness, and edamame is effortlessly crunchy and fun.

INGREDIENTS

4 LARGE SHALLOTS,
peeled

4 CLOVES GARLIC,
peeled

2 TABLESPOONS PEELED AND SLICED
FRESH GINGER

1 TEASPOON TURMERIC

1 TEASPOON CORIANDER SEED

1 LARGE RED CHILE
seeded

¼ CUP RAW CASHEWS

1 TEASPOON DARK MISO

4 CUPS VEGETABLE STOCK

1 CUP CARROT JUICE

1 TABLESPOON TAMARIND PULP

4 OUNCES CAULIFLOWER FLORETS

4 OUNCES GREEN BEANS,
trimmed and chopped

2 MEDIUM CARROTS,
julienned

2 CUPS EDAMAME,
shelled

1 CUP BLACK RICE,
cooked

CILANTRO LEAVES,
stems removed

1 In a coffee grinder or good blender, grind the shallots, garlic, ginger, turmeric, coriander, chile, cashews, and miso to a paste. In a large wok or soup pot over medium heat, whisk the paste with a bit of the vegetable stock until smooth. Gradually whisk in all of the stock and the carrot juice. Add the tamarind pulp and bring to a simmer.

2 Add the cauliflower, green beans, carrots, and edamame and cook to desired tenderness, about 5 minutes for crisp-tender. Serve over black rice in bowls. Sprinkle cilantro on top.

MOROCCAN SQUASH TAGINE

with GARBANZOS *and* COUSCOUS

SERVES 6

Tagine refers to the covered cooking vessel in which a dish like this would be prepared as well as the dish itself. You can use a heavy covered brazier or Dutch oven. This sweet and hearty version has slow-cooked whole shallots and garlic, prunes and squash chunks bathed in spices, and crunchy almonds.

INGREDIENTS

3 TABLESPOONS EXTRA-VIRGIN OLIVE OIL

10 SMALL SHALLOTS,
peeled

8 MEDIUM CLOVES GARLIC,
peeled

1½ POUNDS (4 CUPS) WINTER SQUASH,
peeled and sliced

¼ CUP SLIVERED RAW ALMONDS

12 LARGE PITTED PRUNES,
halved

2 TABLESPOONS SLIVERED LEMON ZEST
(from 1 large lemon)

1 TABLESPOON GRATED FRESH GINGER

1 CUP VEGETABLE STOCK

ONE 15-OUNCE CAN GARBANZO BEANS,
drained and rinsed

1 TABLESPOON HONEY *or* AGAVE SYRUP

½ TEASPOON CINNAMON

1 PINCH SAFFRON,
crushed

SALT

CAYENNE

½ CUP CHOPPED FRESH PARSLEY

COUSCOUS

1½ CUPS VEGETABLE STOCK *or* WATER

1 CUP WHOLE WHEAT INSTANT COUSCOUS

½ TEASPOON OLIVE OIL

½ TEASPOON SALT

1 In a Dutch oven or other heavy pot with a lid over low heat, heat the olive oil and sauté the shallots and garlic. Cook until they are golden and sweet, at least 10 minutes. Add the squash to the pot and continue sautéing, stirring, until the squash browns on the edges. Add the almonds, prunes, slivered lemon zest, and ginger and cook until the almonds start to color. Add the vegetable stock, garbanzo beans, honey, cinnamon, and saffron and cover the pot. Bring to a simmer, cover, and simmer for 10 minutes.

2 When the vegetables in the tagine are tender when pierced with a paring knife, the soup is done. Season with salt and cayenne and sprinkle in parsley. Serve the tagine over the couscous.

3 **To make couscous:** In a small heavy saucepan, bring the vegetable stock to a boil. Add the couscous, olive oil, and the salt. Stir, cover, and remove from the heat. Let stand for 10 minutes, then uncover and fluff with a fork. Cover to keep warm until serving time.

SUMMER TOMATO GAZPACHO

with SILKEN TOFU *and* AVOCADO

SERVES 4

Creamy silken tofu takes two forms in this summery soup: puréed in the tomato base and in tiny cubes that you can crush on your tongue as you savor the crunchy vegetables. Use the best, ripest tomatoes for this—you may have to wait for summer to come!

INGREDIENTS

1 PACKAGE SILKEN FIRM TOFU,
gently pressed

3 TABLESPOONS EXTRA-VIRGIN OLIVE OIL

2 CLOVES GARLIC,
chopped

3 TABLESPOONS LIME JUICE

2 TABLESPOONS LEMON JUICE

1 TEASPOON SALT

FRESHLY GROUND BLACK PEPPER

2½ POUNDS HEIRLOOM TOMATOES,
seeded and diced

½ SMALL CUCUMBER,
seeded and diced

¼ CUP DICED RED ONION

¼ CUP DICED YELLOW BELL PEPPER

¼ CUP MINCED FRESH BASIL

1 LARGE AVOCADO

12 LARGE BASIL LEAVES
(optional)

1 Divide the tofu in half. Put one half in the blender and process, scraping down the sides and repeating until smooth. Add the olive oil, garlic, 2 tablespoons of the lime juice, lemon juice, the salt, and a grinding of pepper and process until smooth. Put the tomatoes and cucumber in the blender with the tofu and pulse just to mix and break up some of the tomatoes—don't purée. Scrape out the mixture into a bowl and stir in the red onion, yellow bell pepper, and minced basil. Dice the remaining half of the tofu and fold in.

2 Cut the avocado in half, remove the pit, and then use a paring knife to cut the flesh into small squares inside the shell. Use a spoon to scoop out the diced flesh. Drizzle the remaining 1 tablespoon of lime juice over the diced avocado. Fold half of the avocado into the gazpacho. Serve the gazpacho, topped with a spoonful of the remaining avocado and some whole basil leaves, if desired.

UNIVERSAL UMAMI BROTH AND SEASONAL JAPANESE CLEAR SOUPS

SERVES 4

Japanese clear soups are an exercise in subtle flavoring and respect for seasonal foods. In this broth, ingredients that are high in umami, the natural chemicals that give foods a sense of meatiness and fullness that is very important in Japanese cuisine, are used instead of fish. Though Parmesan is not Japanese, it is very high in umami and makes the broth delicious; if you are ovo-lactarian, use it. Use the best seasonal vegetables in this broth.

INGREDIENTS
½ OUNCE KOMBU

4 LARGE (½ OUNCE) DRIED
SHIITAKE MUSHROOMS

4 SLICES FRESH GINGER

1 PARMESAN RIND
(optional)

4 TABLESPOONS WHITE MISO

2 TABLESPOONS WHITE TEA LEAVES

2 TABLESPOONS TAMARI

SESAME OIL

WINTER
2 CUPS CUBED KABOCHA SQUASH

4 LEAVES KALE, *sliced thinly across the leaf*

2 LARGE SCALLIONS, *sliced diagonally*
SPRING
4 OUNCES RAW ENOKI MUSHROOMS

8 SPEARS ASPARAGUS TIPS

4 BABY CARROTS, *quartered lengthwise*
SUMMER
2 SMALL ROMA TOMATOES, *seeded and sliced*

4 OUNCES FRENCH BEANS, *stems removed*

1 SMALL YELLOW SQUASH, *sliced*
FALL
1 SMALL SWEET POTATO, *cubed*

4 LEAVES SWISS CHARD, *sliced thinly across the leaf*

1 SMALL DAIKON, *julienned*

1 Place the kombu, shiitakes, ginger, Parmesan rind (if using), and 18 cups of water in a large pot and let stand for 2 hours. Place the pot over low heat until the broth begins to bubble a tiny bit. Remove the kombu and discard, and bring the contents to a simmer for 5 minutes. Remove the pot from the heat, stir in the miso and tea leaves, and steep for 4 minutes. Strain the liquid through a mesh strainer into a pitcher or large glass measuring cup. Let cool completely, or chill overnight.

....

2 Carefully strain the cooled broth through a coffee filter placed in the mesh strainer, pouring the clear liquid off the solids that have collected in the bottom of the pitcher. Discard the solids. Transfer the liquid to a medium pan and warm over low heat. Add the tamari and a few drops of sesame oil.

....

3 Cut the vegetables for your season into beautiful pieces and carefully steam them (if necessary) individually until just done. Compose the vegetables in each of 4 bowls and ladle the warm broth around them. Serve with chopsticks, and drink the broth to finish your meal.

VIETNAMESE PHO

with T O F U

SERVES 4

The key to this soup is making a stock that is redolent of anise and cinnamon, ginger and mushrooms. At a pho restaurant, the thinly sliced vegetables and noodles are served in a large bowl, and the hot stock is ladled over them at the table, cooking them just a little and filling the air with their scent. Herbs and lots of chiles are served on the side, to be added to taste. It is traditional to use green chiles in this, but if you want a little color contrast, use red.

INGREDIENTS

2 TEASPOONS VEGETABLE OIL

2 INCHES FRESH GINGER,
sliced

1 LARGE ONION,
sliced with the skin on

1 LARGE CARROT,
coarsely chopped

2 STALKS CELERY,
coarsely chopped

2 OUNCES DRIED MUSHROOMS

1 CINNAMON STICK

6 STAR ANISE PODS

2 TABLESPOONS TAMARI

1 TEASPOON SALT

ONE 1-INCH CHUNK CHINESE ROCK SUGAR
or 1 TABLESPOON BROWN SUGAR

1 POUND FIRM TOFU,
drained and pressed

8 OUNCES FLAT RICE NOODLES

2 LARGE SERRANO PEPPERS,
thinly sliced

1 CUP THAI BASIL,
torn

¼ CUP HALVED AND SLICED SCALLIONS

2 LARGE LIMES,
cut into wedges

2 CUPS BEAN SPROUTS

½ CUP CILANTRO

3 LARGE JALAPEÑOS,
chopped

SOY SAUCE

1 In a large pot over medium-high heat, heat the oil and sauté the ginger, onion, carrot, and celery until golden. Add 3 quarts of cold water and bring to a simmer. Add the mushrooms, cinnamon, star anise, tamari, and salt. Keep at lowest simmer for 3 hours. Strain, stir in the rock sugar and put in a pan over very low heat.

....

2 Put on a large pot of water to boil. Cut tofu into thin slices, then stack them and cut into bite-size pieces.

....

3 Put the noodles in the boiling water until tender, then drain. Bring the stock back to a simmer.

....

4 In individual wide soup bowls, portion noodles, then arrange the tofu, serranos, Thai basil, and scallions on top. Ladle 1½ to 2 cups of hot stock over the contents of each bowl at the table. Diners squeeze limes into the soup, and add the bean sprouts, cilantro, jalapeños, and soy sauce to taste.

CHAPTER 4

MAIN COURSES

ENTRÉES ARE THE FINAL FRONTIER FOR MEAT EATERS. If you love a carnivore, try these recipes and see if you can work in some meatless meals, to show how good they can be. If there is a difference between the way vegetarians make food and the way omnivores do, it is in approach, not techniques. We still build an entrée around some kind of protein, but the plants invade every dish on the table. Vegetables and fruits abound, with none of the separation of the meat/veg/starch construct that makes standard meat meals so boring. Start with the produce and ask what's good right now, then go home and find a dish to make the most of it.

A fun part of going veg in America is the adventure of discovering cuisines that were already plant based and filled with flavor for centuries. When vegetarians look for a restaurant to visit, Indian, Chinese, Middle Eastern, Japanese, and even Italian eateries have been our options all along. When we cook at home, we can take it even further and use the flavors and spices of these cuisines to make their meat dishes with our chosen proteins. Many of these cuisines use such flavorful spicing and balances of sweet, sour, salty, and umami that they are absolutely satisfying as vegan dishes. Just don't call them vegan when you serve them to your meat-eating guests.

BAKED CREAMY SQUASH PASTA

with ARUGULA

SERVES 4

Tomato sauce is fine, most of the time. But even tastier is a creamy sauce made with squash and chèvre; serve it in a pasta *al forno*. This recipe calls for kabocha squash, but butternut or others will do—they are just a little more moist, so use 2 tablespoons less stock with them.

INGREDIENTS

1 SMALL KABOCHA, RED KURI,
or BUTTERNUT SQUASH

1 TABLESPOON OLIVE OIL

½ CUP DICED ONION

2 CLOVES GARLIC,
chopped

1 TABLESPOON CHOPPED FRESH SAGE

½ CUP WHITE WINE

2 CUPS (2½ OUNCES) ARUGULA

½ CUP VEGETABLE STOCK

1 TEASPOON SALT

4 OUNCES CHÈVRE,
at room temperature

2 CUPS (6 OUNCES)
TUBULAR PASTA, FUSILLI,
or MACARONI

¼ CUP SHREDDED PARMESAN CHEESE

2 TABLESPOONS
CHOPPED WALNUTS

1 Preheat the oven to 375°F. Halve, seed, and bake the squash for about 40 minutes, or until tender when pierced with a paring knife. Let the squash cool, then purée it, reserving 1 cup for this recipe.

2 Put on a large pot of salted water to boil for the pasta. In a large sauté pan over medium heat, heat the olive oil and sauté the onion until tender, about 5 minutes. Add the garlic and sage, and cook until both are golden. Add the wine and bring to a boil. Add the arugula and toss it in the pan to wilt. In a large bowl, whisk together the vegetable stock, the 1 cup puréed squash, and the salt. Add the mixture to the pan. Heat until barely bubbling, then remove from the heat and stir in the chèvre until melted.

3 Cook the pasta in the boiling water according to package directions, testing a minute sooner than the package says, to make sure the pasta is just al dente. Drain well and toss with the reserved squash mixture. Transfer the pasta mixture to a 2-quart casserole and top with the Parmesan and walnuts. Bake for 20 minutes. Serve hot.

BLACK AND GREEN SOY AND CHEESE QUESADILLAS

with SWEET POTATO SALSA

SERVES 3

Here's a tip: Always keep a pack of tortillas in the freezer to make quesadillas for quick weeknight meals. This is a tasty wintertime version, complete with a zesty Sweet Potato Salsa that will wake your slumbering taste buds.

INGREDIENTS

SWEET POTATO SALSA

1 CLOVE GARLIC,
peeled

½ CUP CILANTRO LEAVES,
washed and dried

1 CUP BAKED AND MASHED SWEET POTATO

2 TABLESPOONS LIME JUICE

2 TABLESPOONS
EXTRA-VIRGIN OLIVE OIL
(optional)

1 PINCH RED PEPPER FLAKES

½ TEASPOON SALT

QUESADILLAS

½ CUP SHELLED EDAMAME

½ CUP CANNED BLACK SOYBEANS,
rinsed, and drained

⅛ TEASPOON SALT

1 MEDIUM CHIPOTLE
PEPPER IN ADOBO,
minced

1½ CUPS SHREDDED MANCHEGO *or*
OTHER AGED CHEESE

SIX 6-INCH WHOLE WHEAT TORTILLAS

1 **To make the salsa:** With the machine running, drop the garlic down the feed tube of the food processor. When it is minced, add the cilantro and process to mince. Add the sweet potato, lime juice, olive oil (if using), red pepper flakes, and salt, and process until smooth. Scrape out into a bowl for serving.

2 **To prepare the quesadillas:** In a medium bowl, coarsely mash the edamame, soybeans, salt, and chipotle. Add the cheese and toss to mix. On the cutting board, lay out 3 tortillas. Divide the filling mixture among them, and spread it out to about ½ inch from the edge. Top each with another tortilla.

3 Place a large cast-iron skillet on the stove and heat the skillet on high for 1 minute. Carefully transfer one of your tortilla stacks to the pan and cook until the tortilla is toasted, pressing down on the top with a spatula to encourage adhesion. It should take 1 to 2 minutes per side. Flip the quesadilla with a spatula and cook the other side. Slide the finished quesadilla onto the cutting board and cut it into 6 wedges. Transfer to a plate and keep warm by putting a pan lid over it, slightly ajar.

4 When all the quesadillas are cooked, serve hot with the salsa.

BRAISED GARLIC-SQUASH TART

with AGED GOUDA

MAKES ONE 12-INCH TART / SERVES 6

The lusty flavors of braised squash, aged Gouda, and toasted hazelnuts make this tart irresistible. Kabocha, sometimes called "Japanese pumpkin," is a dark orange, low-moisture squash that holds up well for this, but red kuri or Hubbard squash would do just as well. For a light meal, serve with a green salad.

INGREDIENTS

TART SHELL

1 CUP UNBLEACHED FLOUR

½ CUP CORNMEAL

½ TEASPOON SALT

½ STICK BUTTER,
chilled

½ CUP ICE WATER

FILLING

1½ POUNDS KABOCHA SQUASH,
peeled and cubed

2 MEDIUM SHALLOTS,
chopped

2 TABLESPOONS
EXTRA-VIRGIN OLIVE OIL

4 CLOVES GARLIC,
chopped

½ CUP WHITE WINE

¼ TEASPOON SALT

4 OUNCES AGED GOUDA CHEESE,
shredded

¼ CUP TOASTED HAZELNUTS,
skins rubbed off, coarsely chopped
(see page 93)

1 **To make the tart shell:** In a large bowl, mix the flour, cornmeal, and salt. Using the coarse holes of a grater, shred the butter into the flour mixture and toss it with your fingers to coat. Cut until the mixture is full of coarse lumps. Quickly stir in the ice water just until the dough sticks together, then form the dough into a ball. Chill for 1 hour.

2 Preheat oven to 400°F. Roll out dough and fit into a 12-inch tart pan. Prick the shell all over and bake until edges are browned, about 10 minutes. Let cool on a cooling rack.

3 **To make the filling:** Sauté the squash and shallots in the olive oil in a large pan over medium-high heat, stirring. After 5 minutes, add the garlic and stir. Add the wine and salt and cover for 5 minutes, checking at the end to see if the pan is dry. When the squash is tender when pierced with a paring knife, uncover and cook until the liquids have evaporated. Remove from the heat and let cool.

4 Sprinkle some cheese in the shell and top with the squash mixture, the remaining cheese, and hazelnuts. Bake until the cheese is melted and golden on top, about 20 minutes. Slice in 6 wedges and serve warm.

CRACKER-CRUST PIZZA AL AGLIO

with GOAT CHEESE

MAKES 4 PIZZAS

Restaurants started serving these superthin, crisp pizzas a few years back, and they are a nice change from the thick and doughy ones. You need a pizza stone, and if you get a larger rectangular one, you can make two of these at once. The dough is quick and the baking time is short, so the time spent making the thin-thin crust is balanced out. Top this with any number of toppings, just go very lightly.

INGREDIENTS

1 CUP UNBLEACHED FLOUR

1 CUP WHOLE WHEAT PASTRY FLOUR

1½ TEASPOONS QUICK-RISE YEAST

1 TEASPOON SALT,
plus more to taste

¼ CUP MILK

¾ CUP WARM WATER

36 CLOVES GARLIC,
peeled

1 TEASPOON OLIVE OIL

1 TABLESPOON EXTRA-VIRGIN OLIVE OIL

1 CUP CRUSHED MUIR GLEN
FIRE-ROASTED TOMATOES,
or TOMATO PURÉE

½ TEASPOON RED PEPPER FLAKES

6 LEAVES FRESH BASIL,
plus more for garnish

CORNMEAL

8 OUNCES CHÈVRE

8 TABLESPOONS PARMESAN CHEESE

1 Mix ½ cup of the unbleached flour, ½ cup of the whole wheat pastry flour, the yeast, and the 1 teaspoon salt in the bowl of a stand mixer. Pour in the milk and water and, using the dough hook, beat for 2 minutes. Gradually mix in the remaining flours. Strive for a very pliable dough that is neither sticky nor stiff. Knead the dough for 5 minutes, then place it in an oiled bowl and cover with plastic wrap or a damp towel. Let rise for 30 minutes in a warm spot. Punch down, then let rise for 15 minutes more.

2 Place a pizza stone in the cold oven and preheat the oven to 400°F. Place the garlic on a square of foil. Drizzle with the olive oil and crimp the foil to make a package. Place in the oven and roast for 30 minutes, shaking every 10 minutes. When the garlic is butter-soft and lightly browned, remove to a rack and cool. Keep the oven at 400°F.

3 In a small saucepan over heat, heat the extra-virgin olive oil, add the tomatoes, and bring to a simmer. Simmer for 5 minutes, then add the red pepper flakes, and basil, and season with salt. Let cool.

4 Spread a light coating of cornmeal on your pizza paddle. Punch down the dough and divide it into 4 pieces. On an unfloured counter, roll each piece of dough as thinly as you can. Alternate rolling with picking it up and stretching it carefully over the backs of your hands. Transfer to the paddle and slide it onto the hot stone. Bake for 3 minutes.

5 Remove the crust from the oven and quickly spread on one-quarter of the sauce and top with one-quarter of the garlic cloves and one-quarter of the cheeses. Return the pizza to the stone for 10 minutes more. Remove it to a cutting board, scatter with some torn basil leaves for garnish, slice it in wedges, and serve immediately. Repeat with the remaining ingredients to make 3 more pizzas.

BUDDHA'S DELIGHT

with TOFU SKIN, MOCK ABALONE, *and* TREE EARS

SERVES 6

This is a sentimental favorite, as most vegetarians have eaten a version of this at Chinese restaurants. It is a Chinese New Year tradition with an auspicious number of healing ingredients. You can use arame seaweed instead of hair vegetable, and jujube dates are suggested instead of the traditional dried tiger lily flowers.

INGREDIENTS

½ OUNCE DRIED SHIITAKE MUSHROOMS

8 MEDIUM DRIED TREE EAR MUSHROOMS

1 CUP DRIED WHITE FUNGUS

½ CUP HAIR VEGETABLE

3 STICKS DRIED TOFU SHEETS,
about 8 inches long

½ CUP JUJUBE DATES, GOJI BERRIES,
or WOLFBERRIES

4 OUNCES OYSTER MUSHROOMS,
sliced

4 OUNCES SNOW PEAS,
trimmed

1 LARGE CARROT,
julienned

ONE 8-OUNCE CAN BAMBOO SHOOTS,
rinsed

4 OUNCES MARINATED TOFU,
drained, pressed, and cut into thin slices

ONE 14-OUNCE CAN MOCK ABALONE
or MOCK DUCK,
drained

¼ CUP SOY SAUCE

2 TABLESPOONS SUGAR

½ CUP SHAOXING RICE WINE

1 TABLESPOON RICE VINEGAR

2 TABLESPOONS CORNSTARCH

2 TEASPOONS VEGETABLE OIL

4 CLOVES GARLIC,
chopped

1-INCH FRESH GINGER,
finely julienned

2 TEASPOONS HOT SESAME OIL

2 CUPS BROWN, BLACK, OR RED RICE,
cooked

1 Soak the dried vegetables, tofu, and dates separately in hot water. Clean, rinse, and slice the shiitake and tree ear mushrooms. Set aside ½ cup of the mushroom soaking water. Cut off the tough parts of the fungus and tree ears and cut or tear them into bite-size pieces. Squeeze out the tofu sheets and cut them into bite-size pieces. Combine the rehydrated vegetables and tofu in a large bowl and set aside.

....

2 Put the oyster mushrooms, snow peas, carrot, bamboo shoots, sliced marinated tofu, and mock abalone in a large bowl. Set aside. In a 2-cup measuring cup, whisk the soy sauce, sugar, reserved ½ cup mushroom water, rice wine, rice vinegar, and cornstarch. Set aside.

....

3 Heat a large wok over high heat. When hot, add the vegetable oil and swirl to coat the pan. Add the garlic and ginger, stir for a few seconds, and add the bowl of ingredients from Step 2. Stir just until softened, about 2 minutes, then add the remaining bowl of ingredients from Step 1 and stir. Stir-fry until heated through and the peas are bright green, about 4 minutes. Whisk the soy sauce mixture and pour it into the center of the pan. Stir-fry until the sauce is thick and glossy.

....

4 Sprinkle with the hot sesame oil and serve over cooked rice.

FRENCH LENTIL CASSOULET

SERVES 4

Classic cassoulet is made from lamb, and the lentils are served alongside it. This simply flavored dish makes a hearty winter supper, adorned with a topping of thriftily repurposed extra bread and walnuts.

INGREDIENTS

1 CUP FRENCH LENTILS,
sorted and cleaned

1 WHOLE BAY LEAF

4 TABLESPOONS BUTTER

1 SMALL JAPANESE EGGPLANT,
cubed (about 1½ cups)

1 LARGE ONION,
julienned

1 MEDIUM CARROT,
chopped

1 MEDIUM POTATO,
cubed

2 TABLESPOONS CHOPPED FRESH ROSEMARY

1 MEDIUM ZUCCHINI,
thinly sliced

4 CLOVES GARLIC,
minced

½ TEASPOON CELERY SEED

½ CUP WHITE WINE

2 CUPS CANNED TOMATOES

½ TEASPOON SALT

½ CUP CHOPPED PARSLEY

FRESHLY CRACKED BLACK PEPPER

CRUMB TOPPING

3 CLOVES GARLIC,
peeled

3 TABLESPOONS EXTRA-VIRGIN OLIVE OIL

1 CUP WALNUTS

3 CUPS FRESH WHOLE WHEAT BREADCRUMBS

1 TABLESPOON CHOPPED FRESH THYME

1 Cook the lentils with the bay leaf in a small saucepan over medium heat for 30 minutes. When tender but not falling apart, drain, reserving 1 cup of the cooking liquid. Discard the bay leaf.

2 In a large pot over medium-high heat, melt the butter and sauté the eggplant, onion, carrot, and potato with the rosemary, stirring often. Add the zucchini, garlic, and celery seed and sauté until tender. Add the wine, tomatoes, salt, cooked lentils, and enough of the lentil cooking liquid to make a stew. Bring to a simmer and cook until the potato is tender, 10 to 15 minutes. Stir in parsley and season with pepper.

3 **To make the crumb topping:** Pulse the garlic and olive oil in a food processor until the garlic is minced. Add the walnuts and pulse to chop finely. Add the breadcrumbs and thyme and pulse to mix well. Pour into a cast-iron or nonstick skillet over medium heat and stir, until browned and crisp, about 5 minutes. Put the topping on the cassoulet just before serving.

GARLICKY ROASTED POTATOES

with SPINACH, GREEN OLIVES, *and* PINE NUTS

SERVES 4

Instead of pasta, this entrée starts with a pan of crispy roasted new potatoes and builds on it, layering in spinach, olives, and pine nuts to make a deeply satisfying dish.

INGREDIENTS

1 POUND FINGERLING NEW POTATOES
(or other small new potato)

3 TABLESPOONS EXTRA-VIRGIN OLIVE OIL

COARSE SALT

COARSELY CRACKED BLACK PEPPER

8 OUNCES SPINACH

2 CLOVES GARLIC,
minced

1 CUP ITALIAN GREEN OLIVES,
pitted and sliced

¼ CUP LEMON JUICE

½ CUP PINE NUTS,
toasted

1 Preheat the oven to 400°F. Slice the fingerling potatoes in half lengthwise. Place into a heavy roasting pan, and drizzle with 2 tablespoons of the oil and sprinkle with salt and pepper. Roast for 20 minutes, stir, and depending on the size of the potatoes, roast for 10 to 20 minutes more until browned and crisp.

2 Stem and wash the spinach, then chop coarsely. Heat a large skillet over medium-high heat, then add the remaing 1 tablespoon of olive oil. Add the garlic and stir until fragrant, then drop the damp greens in and toss just to wilt. Add the potatoes and olives and toss to combine. Serve drizzled with lemon juice and sprinkled with the pine nuts.

GOAT CHEESE GNOCCHI
in LEMON–BROCCOLI RABE SAUCE

SERVES 5

Potato is not the only thing used to make the pillowy dumplings called gnocchi. Ricotta is another classic base, so why not take it a delectable step further with chèvre? These are rich and filling, and craveably tangy and tender from the creamy cheese. The trick to great gnocchi is not adding too much flour—always test the recipe by cooking a single gnocco before forming the whole batch!

INGREDIENTS

LEMON–BROCCOLI RABE SAUCE

2 TABLESPOONS
EXTRA-VIRGIN OLIVE OIL

1 CUP CHOPPED ONION

1 STALK CELERY,
chopped

1 MEDIUM CARROT,
chopped

3 CUPS CHOPPED BROCCOLI RABE

1 CUP VEGETABLE STOCK

½ LARGE LEMON,
lemon juice to taste

SALT

FRESHLY CRACKED BLACK PEPPER

2 LARGE EGGS

1 TEASPOON SALT

1 CUP UNBLEACHED FLOUR

1 POUND CHÈVRE,
at room temperature

OLIVE OIL

PARMESAN CHEESE,
freshly grated

1 **To make the sauce:** In a large skillet, over medium-high heat, heat the olive oil and sauté the onion, celery, and carrot. Reduce the heat to low and cook, stirring occasionally, for 10 to 25 minutes, or if you have time, up to 30 minutes to fully caramelize the onion. Add the broccoli rabe and just enough stock to cover. Simmer until all vegetables are very soft, then purée them in a food processor or blender, and add the lemon juice and season with salt and pepper. Keep warm.

....

2 With a potato masher or big spoon, mix the eggs, salt, and ½ cup of the flour into the chèvre. Gradually add flour to make a very soft, slightly sticky dough. Chill for 30 minutes. Bring a pot of salted water to a boil. Spread flour onto the counter and lightly over a baking sheet. Pinch off a 1-inch piece of dough and roll it in flour to make a ball, then shake off excess flour. Drop the single gnocco into the boiling water and wait 1 minute, then gently stir to make sure it is not stuck to the bottom. When the ball floats, take it out with a slotted spoon and let cool slightly, then taste. If the gnocco falls apart, or if it is so soft that it turns to mush, add more flour to the dough. If the gnocco is tender, proceed with forming the rest of the dough. If desired, press each against the tines of a fork to make the characteristic markings and place them on the floured baking sheet. Drop 12 or so gnocchi into the boiling water at a time. As they come to the surface, take them out with slotted spoon. Put the gnocchi into a casserole dish and drizzle with the oil, shaking gently to distribute.

....

3 Reheat the sauce. Carefully toss with the gnocchi and taste for salt and pepper. Top with grated Parmesan and serve.

GRILLED VEGETABLE SFORMATO

SERVES 8

This layered sformato is pretty and filling enough to be a centerpiece main dish.
It can be made a day ahead and reheated, or made a few weeks ahead and frozen,
then thawed overnight in the refrigerator before reheating in the oven at 350°F.

INGREDIENTS

3 LARGE YELLOW BELL PEPPERS,
or JARRED ROASTED YELLOW PEPPERS

½ CUP OLIVE OIL

2 LARGE EGGPLANTS,
thinly sliced lengthwise

4 LARGE EGGS,
lightly beaten

2 CUPS RICOTTA CHEESE

6 OUNCES ROMANO CHEESE,
shredded

4 OUNCES FONTINA CHEESE,
shredded

½ TEASPOON SALT

½ TEASPOON FRESHLY
CRACKED BLACK PEPPER

1½ CUPS FRESH BASIL LEAVES,
washed and dried

3 CLOVES GARLIC,
peeled

½ CUP PISTACHIOS,
shelled

1 CUP SUN-DRIED TOMATOES,
rehydrated

¼ TEASPOON CAYENNE PEPER

1½ CUPS WHOLE WHEAT PENNE,
cooked

½ CUP DRY BREADCRUMBS

BASIL LEAVES

1 Preheat the broiler or barbecue grill and roast the bell peppers until skins are blackened. Place them in a small airtight container and close tightly to steam for 15 minutes. When cool enough to handle, peel, dice, and drain the peppers in a mesh colander, pressing out excess moisture. (If using jarred peppers, drain, rinse, and chop them.)

2 Brush an 11-inch springform pan with some of the olive oil, then set aside. Heat a grill pan or use the grill. Brush the eggplant with olive oil. Grill the slices until tender and decorated with black grill marks (running lengthwise), 2 to 3 minutes on each side. Put a small slice in the center of the springform pan. Lay slices in a fan or flower design covering the bottom and sides and leaving an inch or so hanging over the edges to wrap around the top of the filled pan.

3 In a large bowl, mix the eggs, cheeses, salt, and pepper. Remove half of the mixture to another bowl. Use a food processor to finely grind the basil, garlic, and pistachios, then mix it with half of the cheese mixture. Dice the tomatoes and add it to the other half of the cheese mixture, then mix in the cayenne. Divide the cooked pasta between the two bowls and fold the contents of each bowl together gently.

4 Preheat the oven to 400°F. Into the eggplant-lined pan, sprinkle 2 tablespoons of the breadcrumbs and distribute the pasta and tomato mixture. Level the surface and top with the yellow bell peppers and another 2 tablespoons crumbs. Top with remaining pasta mixture, level, and cover with the remaining crumbs. Fold the overhanging eggplant back onto the top of the peppers.

5 Bake for 50 to 60 minutes and let stand for 20 minutes before serving to firm up. Run a sharp knife around edge of pan. Invert the pan onto a serving plate and release springform, carefully removing bottom. Garnish with the basil and serve.

GREEK VEGETABLE FETA PIE

in PHYLLO

SERVES 6

Phyllo pastry made with olive oil is light and flavorful, it just doesn't get quite as crisp as phyllo made with butter. This pie is filled with tender roasted vegetables and crunchy pistachios, a nice change from spinach.

INGREDIENTS

½ SMALL (ABOUT ¾ POUND) EGGPLANT,
chopped into 1-inch cubes

1 MEDIUM ZUCCHINI,
chopped into 1-inch cubes

1 LARGE ONION,
chopped

1 TABLESPOON OLIVE OIL

1 BUNCH SWISS CHARD,
washed, dried, stemmed, and chopped

3 CLOVES GARLIC,
minced

8 OUNCES GOAT *or* SHEEP FETA CHEESE,
drained

2 LARGE EGGS,
lightly beaten

½ CUP COARSELY CHOPPED PISTACHIOS

½ TEASPOON OREGANO

½ TEASPOON DILL

½ TEASPOON SALT

½ TEASPOON CRACKED
BLACK PEPPER

8 SHEETS PHYLLO DOUGH,
thawed overnight in the refrigerator

OLIVE OIL SPRAY

1 Preheat the oven to 400°F. In a deep roasting pan, toss the eggplant, zucchini, and onion in the oil. Roast for 20 minutes, stir, and roast for 10 minutes more. Add the chard and garlic. Cover and roast until chard is wilted, about 10 minutes. Remove from oven, stir, and let cool. Leave the oven on. Transfer the vegetables to a large bowl. Add the feta, eggs, pistachios, oregano, dill, salt, and pepper and stir to mix.

2 Place the phyllo on the counter, cover with plastic wrap, and then put a barely damp towel over that, making sure the phyllo is not exposed to air. Quickly layer 4 sheets of phyllo on the prepared pan, coating each one with olive oil spray. Spread the filling mixture over the phyllo, then fold overhanging edges to cover the filling. Layer 4 more sheets of phyllo over the filling, folding them to fit the pan and coating with oil spray. Pat down the phyllo. Bake until golden, 20 to 25 minutes and serve warm.

HAZELNUT "MEATBALLS" AND SAUCE

on top of SPAGHETTI

SERVES 4

Toasty hazelnuts and chunks of carrot make these crispy nuggets a delight to eat, especially with a comforting batch of tomato-drenched spaghetti. Soy Parmesan is one of the soy cheeses that tastes rather like the familiar canned Parm, so if you crave that snowy topping, it works.

INGREDIENTS

"MEATBALLS"

1½ CUPS HAZELNUTS

1 PACKAGE EXTRA-FIRM TOFU,
drained and pressed

½ CUP ROLLED OATS

2 LARGE SCALLIONS,
chopped

1 LARGE CARROT,
peeled and sliced

1½ TABLESPOONS FRESH CHOPPED THYME

1 TEASPOON SALT

1 TEASPOON BALSAMIC VINEGAR

2 TABLESPOONS WHITE MISO

1 TABLESPOON OLIVE OIL

SAUCE

3 TABLESPOONS EXTRA-VIRGIN OLIVE OIL

1 SMALL ONION,
chopped

1 RIB CELERY,
chopped

2 OUNCES MUSHROOMS,
sliced

2 CLOVES GARLIC,
chopped

14 OUNCES FIRE-ROASTED TOMATOES,
crushed

½ CUP DRY RED WINE

¼ TEASPOON RED PEPPER FLAKES

½ CUP FRESH CHOPPED BASIL

½ POUND WHOLE WHEAT SPAGHETTI

PARMESAN *or* SOY PARMESAN
(optional)

1 **To make the "meatballs":** Toast the hazelnuts in a 300°F oven for 10 minutes, then let cool. Rub off the skins, and if any won't come off, toast them for 5 minutes more and try to rub off the skin again. Increase the oven temperature to 400°F. Crumble the tofu into a bowl. In a food processor or blender, purée the oats and hazelnuts until finely chopped, with a few chunks. Add to the tofu. Put the scallions and carrots into the processor bowl and mince. Add the carrot mixture to the tofu with the thyme, salt, vinegar, and miso and mix, crushing the tofu until the mixture holds together. Oil a sheet pan with the olive oil. Form 1- to 1½-inch balls from the tofu mixture. Place them on the pan and bake until they are firm and toasted-looking, about 10 minutes. Then turn them over carefully with a metal spatula and bake 10 minutes more.

2 **To make the sauce:** Heat the extra-virgin olive oil in a 2-quart pot over medium-high heat. Add the onion, celery, and mushrooms and sauté until the onion is soft and tender. Add the garlic and cook until fragrant. Add tomatoes, wine, and red pepper flakes and cook until thickened. Stir in the basil just before serving.

3 Cook the pasta according to the package directions. Toss the hot pasta with half of the sauce. Serve pasta with hazelnut "meatballs" on top and drizzle with remaining sauce. Top with the Parmesan, if desired.

SPICY ITALIAN "MEAT" LOAF

SERVES 8

Make this delicious loaf on Sunday and have it for sandwiches all week long. Black soybeans are a little firmer than other beans and, combined with walnuts, they give the loaf a perfect texture.

INGREDIENTS

LOAF

2 TEASPOONS OLIVE OIL

1 CUP CHOPPED ONION

1 MEDIUM RED BELL PEPPER,
seeded, deribbed, and chopped

1 CUP SHREDDED ZUCCHINI

2 CUPS TOASTED WALNUTS

2 CUPS SOFT WHOLE WHEAT BREADCRUMBS
(or about 4 slices of bread, ground)

TWO 14-OUNCE CANS BLACK SOYBEANS,
drained and rinsed

¼ CUP TAHINI

2 TABLESPOONS NUTRITIONAL YEAST

½ CUP CHOPPED FRESH BASIL

2 TABLESPOONS CHOPPED FRESH THYME

2 TEASPOONS DRIED SAGE

2 TEASPOONS COARSELY CHOPPED FENNEL SEED

¼ CUP CAPERS,
rinsed

1 TEASPOON RED PEPPER FLAKES

½ TEASPOON SALT

OLIVE OIL

¼ CUP TOMATO PASTE

2 TABLESPOONS RED WINE

2 TABLESPOONS HONEY

1 **To make the loaf:** Preheat the oven to 400°F. Heat a large sauté pan over medium-high heat, add the olive oil, and sauté the onion, bell pepper, and zucchini. Lower the heat when they are softened and slightly browned. In a food processor, grind the walnuts to bits, but not powder. Scrape nuts into a large bowl and add the breadcrumbs. (If using sliced bread, grind it in the processor first, then measure.) Add the black soybeans to the processor bowl, and pulse just to coarsely break the beans—don't purée. Add the beans to the bowl with the nuts and stir in the remaining loaf ingredients. Mix with your hands and knead to combine.

2 Lightly oil a loaf pan with olive oil. Press the loaf mixture into the pan and bake for 30 minutes. Stir together the tomato paste, red wine, and honey and spread on the loaf, then return it to the oven for 10 minutes more. Remove the loaf to a rack to cool for at least 10 minutes before slicing and serving.

I-TAL VEGETABLE AND RED BEAN RUNDOWN

MAKES 4 CUPS / SERVES 4

There are many ways to prepare Rundown, the Jamaican celebration of tropical ingredients, all cooked in delicious fresh coconut milk. It's a little bit spicy and a staple of the Rastafarians, who prefer "i-tal" or "vital" vegetarian foods. This version is only slightly spicy, so if you like heat, use the whole chile.

INGREDIENTS

2 TEASPOONS OLIVE OIL

1 CUP CHOPPED ONION

¼ CUP CHOPPED SCALLION

2 TEASPOONS CHOPPED FRESH THYME

2 CLOVES GARLIC,
minced

½ TEASPOON GROUND ALLSPICE

¼ SMALL SCOTCH BONNET CHILE,
minced

1 CUP COCONUT MILK

½ POUND SWEET POTATO,
cubed

1 MEDIUM CARROT,
chopped

½ MEDIUM RED BELL PEPPER,
seeded, deribbed, and chopped

½ CUP VEGETABLE STOCK

2 CUPS CHOPPED CABBAGE

1 EAR SWEET CORN,
kernels cut off

ONE 15-OUNCE CAN RED BEANS,
drained

SALT

FRESHLY GROUND BLACK PEPPER

¼ CUP MINCED CHIVES

1 Heat a 2-quart pot over medium-high heat, add the oil, then sauté the onion, scallion, thyme, garlic, allspice, and chile until the onion is very soft. Add the coconut milk and bring to a simmer, then add the sweet potato, carrot, bell pepper, vegetable stock, cabbage, corn, and beans. Bring to a simmer, then cover and cook until the sweet potato is tender, about 10 minutes. Uncover and simmer until everything is tender and the liquids are creamy and thick. Add water if necessary to keep it from becoming too thick.

2 Season with salt and pepper, then serve in bowls, garnished with the chives.

JAMAICAN VEGGIE PATTIES

MAKES 12

In Jamaica the crust of these irresistible patties is undoubtedly made with lard. But coconut oil is a vegan alternative that makes a flaky and delicious crust. They are simple to make and addictive to eat.

INGREDIENTS

CRUST

1 CUP FLOUR

1 CUP WHOLE WHEAT PASTRY FLOUR

½ TEASPOON TURMERIC

¼ TEASPOON GROUND FENUGREEK

½ TEASPOON SALT

½ CUP COCONUT OIL
(measure and chill until firm)

½ CUP ICE WATER

FILLING

1 TABLESPOON COCONUT OIL

2 CUPS FINELY CHOPPED CABBAGE

1 LARGE CARROT,
chopped

4 CUPS FRESH SPINACH,
washed

2 MEDIUM ROMA TOMATOES,
seeded and diced

4 LARGE SCALLIONS,
chopped

1 LARGE JALAPEÑO,
chopped

¼ TEASPOON ALLSPICE

1 TEASPOON DRIED THYME

½ TEASPOON SALT,
or TO TASTE

1 LARGE EGG,
whisked (optional)

1 **To make the crust:** In a large bowl, mix the flours, turmeric, fenugreek, and salt. Cut in the cold coconut oil, using a pastry blender to distribute the oil into pea-size chunks. Stir in the ice water to make a firm dough. Divide into 12 balls and chill for 30 minutes. Preheat oven to 375°F.

2 **To make the filling:** In a large sauté pan over medium-high heat, heat the coconut oil and sauté the vegetables until tender and dry. Season with the allspice, thyme, and salt. Let cool, and if liquid pools in the bottom, squeeze it out.

3 Roll out the dough rounds into 5-inch ovals and fill with about 3 tablespoons of the cooled filling. Dampen and seal the edges with a fork, then pierce the top once with the fork. Place on an oiled or parchment-lined sheet pan and brush tops with the egg, if desired. Bake until patties are golden brown on the bottoms, about 20 minutes. Serve hot.

JAPANESE CURRY SOBA

with BLACK SOYBEANS

SERVES 4

Curries are everywhere and yet are always a little different. In Japan cooks use a premade curry roux, combining toasted curry spices, thickeners, and lard. Here the flavors of a Japanese curry soup are concentrated in a sauce that coats chewy noodles and crunchy veggies.

INGREDIENTS

2 TABLESPOONS BUTTER *or* OIL

1 SMALL ONION,
chopped

2 CLOVES GARLIC,
chopped

1 TABLESPOON CHOPPED FRESH GINGER

1 TABLESPOON UNBLEACHED FLOUR

1 TABLESPOON MADRAS CURRY POWDER

2 SMALL BABY EGGPLANTS,
cut into ½-inch-thick slices

1 LARGE CARROT,
julienned

1 TABLESPOON TOMATO PASTE

1 TABLESPOON HONEY *or* BROWN SUGAR

½ TEASPOON VEGAN WORCESTERSHIRE SAUCE

1 CUP VEGETABLE STOCK

¼ CUP SHOYU

¼ CUP MIRIN

ONE 15-OUNCE CAN BLACK SOYBEANS,
drained

7 OUNCES SOBA NOODLES,
cooked

4 LARGE SCALLIONS,
slivered

1 In a large skillet or wok over medium heat, heat the butter. Add the onion and sauté until soft, then lower the heat and cook until soft and sweet, about 5 minutes more. Add the garlic, ginger, flour, and curry powder, and stir to mix well. Add the eggplant and carrot and stir over low heat until the roux is toasted, about 2 minutes.

2 Add the tomato paste, honey, Worcestershire sauce, and vegetable stock and stir to mix well. Add the shoyu, mirin, and black soybeans and bring to a simmer. When the sauce is glossy and thick, serve it over the soba noodles, topped with the scallions.

LAOTIAN GREEN CURRY MOCK DUCK

with LONG BEANS *and* NEW POTATOES

MAKES ABOUT 5 CUPS / SERVES 4

Using a Thai green curry paste in this dish is much easier than making a Laotian one from scratch. But adding a few spices and fresh dill shifts the flavor to Laos and gives the lush sauce a fresh herbal flavor.

INGREDIENTS

ONE 10-OUNCE CAN MOCK DUCK

ONE 13.5-OUNCE CAN *(or 1½ cups)* COCONUT MILK

1 TEASPOON GREEN CURRY PASTE

¼ TEASPOON TURMERIC

1 TEASPOON DARK MISO

1 TEASPOON PALM SUGAR

1 TEASPOON SOY SAUCE

6 LARGE LIME LEAVES,
or THE ZEST OF 2 LIMES

1 PINCH SALT

8 OUNCES LONG BEANS *or* FRENCH BEANS,
trimmed and sliced

8 OUNCES FINGERLING NEW POTATOES,
halved or quartered

½ LARGE RED BELL PEPPER,
sliced

1 CUP SHORT-GRAIN BROWN
or BLACK RICE,
cooked

½ CUP COARSELY CHOPPED FRESH DILL

1 Drain the mock duck and squeeze out as much liquid as possible, then set aside. In a wok or large skillet off the heat, pour the coconut milk. Whisk in the curry paste, turmeric, miso, and palm sugar to dissolve. Add the soy sauce, lime leaves, and salt. Turn the heat to high and bring to a simmer.

2 Taste the sauce and add more curry paste if desired—but remember that it will get a little spicier as it cooks. Add the mock duck and vegetables to the pan and bring to a boil. Boil until the potatoes are tender and the sauce thickens, about 8 minutes. Serve over the rice and scatter the dill over the top.

MANGO EGG CURRY

SERVES 4

You may be familiar with the huevos rancheros of Southwestern origin, but have you tried egg curry? This is so much more exciting and is destined to become a fallback meal on weeknights, for lunch, and even for breakfast. It's usually made with tomatoes, not mangoes, but since mangoes lend themselves to spicy curries, why not?

INGREDIENTS

1 TABLESPOON
EXTRA-VIRGIN OLIVE OIL

1 CUP CHOPPED ONION

2 TEASPOONS BROWN MUSTARD SEEDS

1 TEASPOON WHOLE CUMIN SEEDS

1 LARGE JALAPEÑO,
chopped

2 CLOVES GARLIC,
chopped

2 TABLESPOONS CHOPPED FRESH GINGER

½ TEASPOON TURMERIC

1 LARGE RIPE MANGO,
peeled and chopped

8 OUNCES TOMATO SAUCE

¼ TEASPOON SALT

1 TEASPOON LEMON JUICE

4 LARGE EGGS

2 CUPS COOKED BROWN RICE
or 4 SLICES TOAST

4 SPRIGS CILANTRO
(optional)

1 Heat a 12-inch cast-iron skillet over high heat. Add the oil to the hot pan. Add onion, mustard seeds, cumin seed, and jalapeño and stir. Cook until the onions are softened and slightly browned, about 5 minutes. Add the garlic, ginger, and turmeric and cook for 2 minutes more. Add mango, tomato sauce, salt, and lemon juice and cook until thickened, about 3 minutes.

2 Make 4 wells in the mixture in the pan, and crack an egg into each impression. Cover the pan and cook until the whites are cooked and the yolks are slightly runny, 2 to 3 minutes. Serve the curry over rice or toast, 1 egg per person, dividing the sauce among the plates. Garnish each with a cilantro sprig, if desired.

JAVANESE TEMPEH SAMBAL GORENG

MAKES 6 CUPS / SERVES 6

On the island of Java, tempeh is typically deep-fried, then doused in rich, hot curry. But this recipe cuts steps and fat grams by searing the tempeh and then simmering it in a wildly flavorful tomato-coconut sauce.

INGREDIENTS

3 MEDIUM SHALLOTS,
peeled and sliced

2 CLOVES GARLIC,
peeled

2-INCH FRESH GINGER,
sliced

2 LARGE RED JALAPEÑOS,
seeded

1 TEASPOON MISO

2 MACADAMIA NUTS *or* 1 BRAZIL NUT

1 TEASPOON GROUND CORIANDER

1 TEASPOON PAPRIKA

¾ TEASPOON SALT

2 TABLESPOONS TAMARIND PULP

2 TABLESPOONS CANOLA OIL

12 OUNCES TEMPEH,
cut into ½-inch cubes

¾ CUP COCONUT MILK

1 14-OUNCE CAN DICED TOMATOES,
drained (reserve liquid)

1¾ CUPS VEGETABLE STOCK

2 LARGE KAFFIR LIME LEAVES
or ZEST OF 1 LIME

1 STALK LEMONGRASS,
cut into 3-inch pieces

1 CUP BROWN, BLACK *or* RED RICE,
cooked

1 In a food processor, grind the shallots, garlic, ginger, jalapeños, miso, nuts, coriander, paprika, salt, and tamarind. Heat a large skillet or wok over high heat until very hot, then add the oil. Swirl the pan to coat, then add the tempeh and sear. When the tempeh is browned, push it to one side of the pan. In the open space, add the paste from the food processor and stir in a few tablespoons of the coconut milk. Reduce the heat to medium and cook, stirring until the paste darkens and thickens.

2 Add diced tomatoes, ¼ cup of the tomato liquid, the vegetable stock, lime leaves, lemongrass, and remaining coconut milk. Simmer 15 to 20 minutes. If the sauce gets too thick, add more tomato liquid and simmer to get all the lemongrass and lime flavors into the sauce. Serve over rice.

PROVENÇAL CARAMELIZED ONION AND GREENS TART

with HERBS *and* CHÈVRE

SERVES 6

This meal is a great way to honor free-range, grass-fed eggs, as well as eat your greens.
Swiss chard has a distinctive taste and heft, but if you don't have any, use spinach.

INGREDIENTS

2 TABLESPOONS BUTTER

2 MEDIUM ONIONS *(about 3 cups)*,
minced

2 TEASPOONS CHOPPED FRESH THYME

½ POUND SWISS CHARD *or* SPINACH,
washed, stemmed, and chopped

5 LARGE EGGS

¼ CUP MILK

½ TEASPOON SALT

1 TEASPOON FRESHLY
CRACKED BLACK PEPPER

¼ CUP PITTED AND CHOPPED
FRENCH BLACK OLIVES

2 OUNCES CHÈVRE,
crumbled

1 Preheat the oven to 375°F. Use a teaspoon of the butter to butter a 9-inch pie pan. In a large sauté pan over low heat, melt the remaining butter and then sauté the onions, until caramel-colored and shrunken, 45 minutes. Add the thyme and sauté for 1 minute. Add the chopped chard and stir. Cook only until the chard turns bright green and shrinks a bit, about 2 minutes. Remove the pan from the heat and let cool.

2 In a large bowl, whisk the eggs with the milk, salt, and pepper. Distribute the sautéed chard mixture in the prepared pie pan, sprinkle the olives over it, then sprinkle the crumbled chèvre over that. Pour the egg mixture over the filling and wiggle the pan a bit to make sure the eggs reach the bottom of the pan. Bake until the tart is puffed and golden, 25 to 30 minutes. Slice into wedges to serve.

RED LENTIL AND SWEET POTATO SAMOSAS

with TOMATO-APRICOT CHUTNEY

SERVES 8

Potato samosas are usually served as appetizers or snacks, but these are big and hearty enough to sit at the middle of the plate. Packed with spiced red lentils, sweet potatoes, and herbs and wrapped in a tender pastry, they are perfect with a tangy-sweet tomato chutney.

INGREDIENTS

1 CUP UNBLEACHED FLOUR

1 CUP WHOLE WHEAT PASTRY FLOUR

½ TEASPOON SALT

4 TABLESPOONS BUTTER *or* MARGARINE

¾ CUP BUTTERMILK *or* SOYMILK

1½ CUPS CUBED SWEET POTATO

½ CUP RED LENTILS

2 TEASPOONS GHEE *or* MARGARINE

1 TEASPOON BROWN MUSTARD SEEDS

1 TEASPOON CUMIN SEEDS

1 LARGE RED CHILE,
chopped

1 TABLESPOON CHOPPED FRESH GINGER

½ TEASPOON TURMERIC

½ TEASPOON GARAM MASALA

½ CUP FRESH WHOLE WHEAT BREADCRUMBS

½ TEASPOON SALT

1 TEASPOON LEMON JUICE

½ CUP MINCED CILANTRO

½ CUP CHOPPED TOASTED PISTACHIOS

VEGETABLE SPRAY

TOMATO-APRICOT CHUTNEY

1 TEASPOON FENNEL SEEDS

2 TEASPOONS BLACK MUSTARD SEEDS

¼ CUP LEMON JUICE

¼ CUP ORANGE JUICE

2 TABLESPOONS CHOPPED FRESH GINGER

½ TEASPOON CAYENNE

½ CUP DRIED APRICOT HALVES,
chopped

2 TABLESPOONS BROWN SUGAR

1 CUP TOMATO PURÉE

½ TEASPOON SALT

1 In a large bowl, mix both the flours and the salt. Using a grater or pastry cutter, cut in the butter to the size of long-grain rice. Stir in the buttermilk gradually, just until a pliable dough is formed. Divide into 8 pieces and make each into a ball. Cover and let rest at room temperature.

2 In a medium saucepan over high heat, combine the sweet potato and red lentils with 1½ cups water. Bring to a boil and reduce to a simmer. Cover and cook for 25 to 30 minutes, checking occasionally and adding a little more water if they are sticking, but not too much. When the lentils are falling-apart tender, remove the pan from the heat.

3 In a large sauté pan over high heat, heat the ghee and cook the mustard and cumin seeds until they start to pop. Reduce heat to medium and add the chile and ginger and cook for 1 minute, then add the turmeric and garam masala and stir. Add the lentil mixture and the breadcrumbs. The mixture should be very thick—if not, cook, stirring until a scoop of the filling will hold its shape. Stir in the salt, lemon juice, cilantro, and pistachios and let cool.

4 Preheat the oven to 375°F and coat a baking sheet with vegetable spray. Roll out each dough ball into a 4-inch oval and scoop about ¼ cup of the filling in each. Brush the edge with water, fold the dough over, enclosing the filling, and seal with a fork. Place the samosas on the prepared baking sheet and bake until golden brown on the bottoms and edges, about 20 minutes. Serve hot with the chutney.

5 **To make the chutney:** In a small saucepan over medium heat, dry-toast the fennel and mustard seeds until fragrant. Add the lemon and orange juices (careful, they may spatter) and the remaining ingredients. Simmer over low heat until thick, then purée in a food processor. Scrape into a small bowl and let cool. Serve at room temperature.

ROMAN CHICKPEA GNOCCHI GRATIN

with ROASTED SUMMER SQUASH

SERVES 6

This pretty casserole of scalloped gnocchi crescents, scattered with tender roasted veggies, is pure comfort food. Garbanzo flour is used instead of the traditional semolina, adding the nutrients and flavor of beans to a classic side dish.

INGREDIENTS

2 TABLESPOONS BUTTER

3 CUPS WHOLE MILK

2 CUPS GARBANZO FLOUR

1 TEASPOON SALT

2 LARGE EGGS

1 CUP PARMESAN CHEESE

¼ CUP MINCED PARSLEY,
plus 1 sprig for garnish

1 MEDIUM ZUCCHINI

1 MEDIUM YELLOW SQUASH

½ LARGE RED BELL PEPPER,
seeded and deribbed

2 TEASPOONS OLIVE OIL

1 Preheat the oven to 425°F. Use 1 teaspoon of the butter to grease both a baking sheet with ¾-inch-high sides and a large baking dish.

2 In the top of a double boiler, gradually whisk milk into the flour until smooth. Add the salt and the remaining butter. Place over simmering water and cover, stirring every 5 minutes, until it's thick enough for a spoon to stand in. Remove from the heat and whisk in the eggs and ½ cup of the Parmesan cheese. Spread the mixture on the prepared baking sheet to a ½-inch thickness and let cool. When firm, cut out 3-inch-wide crescent moons with a biscuit cutter or glass. Arrange them in the prepared baking dish, overlapping the pieces to look like shingles on a roof, and cover with the parsley and the remaining cheese.

3 Slice the zucchini, squash, and bell pepper into long ½-inch-wide strips, and place them on a sheet pan. Toss the vegetables with the oil and put them in the oven with the gnocchi gratin, putting the gratin on the top shelf. Bake until the gnocchi gratin is a deep golden color and the vegetables are tender and browning, about 15 to 20 minutes. Serve hot. Scatter the roasted veggies down the center of the gratin at serving, and garnish with a parsley sprig.

ROASTED FENNEL, RED PEPPER, AND ARUGULA PASTA

with FETA *and* OLIVES

SERVES 4

Who doesn't love pasta tossed with great olive oil instead of a thick sauce?
Roasted fennel is sweet and soft, a great contrast to tangy feta and olives.
Use your best, most flavorful olive oil.

INGREDIENTS

2 LARGE FENNEL BULBS

1 LARGE RED BELL PEPPER,
seeded, deribbed, and chopped

ZEST OF 1 LARGE LEMON

4 TABLESPOONS CUP OLIVE OIL

5 OUNCES ARUGULA,
washed and chopped

8 OUNCES WHOLE WHEAT PENNE PASTA

2 TABLESPOONS LEMON JUICE

4 OUNCES FETA CHEESE,
crumbled

½ CUP PITTED AND CHOPPED
KALAMATA OLIVES

½ TEASPOON SALT

1 TEASPOON FRESHLY
CRACKED BLACK PEPPER

1 Preheat the oven to 400°F. Clean the fennel. Cut each bulb into 4 vertical pieces and cut crosswise into 1-inch pieces. Discard the stalks. Chop the tips of the leaves to make ½ cup and set aside. In a large roasting pan, toss the fennel pieces, bell pepper, and lemon zest with 2 tablespoons the olive oil and cover tightly with foil. Roast, covered, until tender when pierced with a knife, about 20 minutes, then roast for 10 minutes more uncovered. Stir in the arugula and cover to wilt. Let cool.

2 Cook the pasta and drain. Whisk the remaining 2 tablespoons olive oil with the lemon juice in a small cup. In the pasta pot or a large bowl, toss the pasta with the fennel mixture, reserved fennel greens, feta, olives, lemon mixture, salt, and pepper. Serve hot or cool.

SINGAPORE VEGETABLE CURRY

with MOCK DUCK

SERVES 5

Singapore is the center of an ongoing global fusion, and it's blessed with tropical foods and flavors to spare. This simplified version of a curry can be made with all sorts of vegetables—once you try it out, you can substitute eggplant, potatoes, snow peas, and whatever else seems appetizing.

INGREDIENTS

3 LARGE RED FRESNO CHILES,
seeded, 2 whole, 1 slivered

1 LARGE SHALLOT,
chopped

2 CLOVES GARLIC,
chopped

1 TABLESPOON CHOPPED FRESH GINGER

½ STALK LEMONGRASS,
thinly sliced

2 TABLESPOONS MADRAS CURRY POWDER

½ TEASPOON TURMERIC

⅛ TEASPOON ALLSPICE

½ TEASPOON SALT

1 TABLESPOON OIL

1½ CUPS (1 CAN) COCONUT MILK

1 SMALL RED ONION,
cut into ¾-inch squares

1 CUP SWEET POTATO,
cubed

1 MEDIUM CARROT,
chopped

4 OUNCES FRENCH BEANS,
sliced

10 OUNCES MOCK DUCK *or* SEITAN,
drained and cut into bite-size pieces

12 CHERRY TOMATOES,
halved and seeded

1½ CUPS BROWN, BLACK, *or* RED RICE

1 In a spice grinder or coffee mill, finely grind the 2 whole chiles, the shallot, garlic, ginger, and lemongrass, then add the curry powder, turmeric, allspice, and salt, and grind to mix.

2 Heat a large skillet or cast-iron pan over high heat and add the oil, swirling to coat. Add the curry paste and stir continuously, mashing and toasting the paste until browned in spots. Stir in the coconut milk and bring to a simmer, then add onion, sweet potato, carrot, beans, slivered chile, and mock duck. Cover and cook for 10 minutes. When the sweet potatoes are tender, stir in the tomatoes and heat through.

3 Cook the rice. Taste the curry for salt and heat, and adjust if needed. Serve the curry over the rice.

SZECHUAN TOFU IN SPICY BLACK BEAN SAUCE

with WHOLE WHEAT NOODLES

MAKES ABOUT 4 CUPS / SERVES 4

Black bean sauce is made from fermented black soybeans, not the usual turtle bean. It is a treasure trove of depth of flavor and adds gravitas to a light stir-fry. If you have access to Szechuan peppercorns, try crushing ½ teaspoon and adding it with the vegetables.

INGREDIENTS

1 PACKAGE FIRM TOFU,
drained and pressed

½ CUP PINEAPPLE JUICE

2 TABLESPOONS RICE VINEGAR

TABLESPOONS SHAOXING
RICE WINE *or* SHERRY

2 TABLESPOONS BLACK BEAN
GARLIC SAUCE

1 TABLESPOON HOT SESAME OIL

1 TABLESPOON SOY SAUCE

1 TABLESPOON SWEETENER

1 TABLESPOON CORNSTARCH

1 TABLESPOON CANOLA OIL

½ TEASPOON RED PEPPER FLAKES

4 CUPS CHOPPED BROCCOLINI
or BROCCOLI RABE

2 LARGE CARROTS,
julienned

2 TABLESPOONS FRESH GINGER,
julienned

6 OUNCES COOKED WHOLE-WHEAT SPAGHETTI
or UDON NOODLES

4 SCALLIONS,
thinly sliced

½ CUP DRY-ROASTED PEANUTS,
chopped

1 Slice the tofu block into ⅓-inch-thick slabs and set aside. Mix the pineapple juice, rice vinegar, rice wine, black bean garlic sauce, hot sesame oil, soy sauce, and sweetener in a cup, then whisk in the cornstarch.

2 Heat a large wok or cast-iron skillet over high heat, then add the canola oil and swirl to coat. Toss in the tofu and red pepper flakes and stir-fry until all sides of the tofu are browned. Add the Broccolini and carrots to the pan and stir-fry until the Broccolini is dark green, about 1 minute. Add the ginger and toss for a few seconds. Stir and pour the black bean sauce mixture into the center of the pan. Stir continuously to coat the vegetables. When the sauce is thickened and glossy, remove it from the heat and serve over the noodles. Top with the scallions and peanuts.

INDIVIDUAL VEGGIE-STUFFED TEMPEH TIMBALES

with RED WINE SAUCE

MAKES 6 TIMBALES

During the holidays, vegans and vegetarians often wish for a centerpiece main
course, with all the flavors we associate with turkey and stuffing. This recipe solves
the conundrum deliciously, giving each diner an individual timbale filled with savory
roasted vegetables and drizzled with a deeply reduced red wine sauce.

INGREDIENTS

1 CUP DICED SWEET POTATO

1 CUP DICED PARSNIP

BIG PINCH OF SALT

2 TABLESPOONS EXTRA-VIRGIN OLIVE OIL

1½ CUPS DICED ONION

TWO 8-OUNCE PACKAGES TEMPEH

1 CUP VEGETABLE STOCK

OLIVE OIL SPRAY

1 POUND FIRM TOFU,
drained and pressed

2 TEASPOONS DIJON MUSTARD

1 TEASPOON TAMARI

1 TEASPOON DRIED SAGE

1 TEASPOON DRIED THYME

1/2 TEASPOON SALT

2 TABLESPOONS NUTRITIONAL YEAST

2 TABLESPOONS CORNSTARCH

6 SPRIGS SAGE

RED WINE SAUCE

¾ CUP RED WINE

4 LARGE DRIED SHIITAKE MUSHROOMS

2 MEDIUM SUN-DRIED TOMATOES

1 LARGE BAY LEAF

1½ TEASPOONS CORNSTARCH

2 TABLESPOONS AGAVE SYRUP *or* HONEY

SALT

1 Preheat the oven to 400°F. Toss the sweet potato, parsnip, salt, and 1 tablespoon
of the olive oil in a 9-inch baking pan. Tightly cover and roast for 30 minutes.
Sauté the onions in remaining 1 tablespoon olive oil, stirring occasionally, until
the onions are sweet and golden. In a food processor, grind the tempeh to the con-
sistency of coarse breadcrumbs. Add the ground tempeh to the onion sauté and
cook, stirring, over medium-high heat, until lightly browned. Add the vegetable
stock and cook, stirring, until absorbed and dry. Remove from heat and let cool.

2 Spray a coating of oil in six 1-cup ramekins and set aside. In a mixing bowl,
crush the tofu with your hands and add the cooked tempeh mixture, mustard,
tamari, sage, thyme, salt, nutritional yeast, and cornstarch. Mix thoroughly by
squeezing and kneading it in your hands. Scoop ¼ cup of the mixture into each
ramekin and then place a heaping tablespoon of sweet potato and parsnip in
the center. Cover with the tempeh mixture and smooth the tops. Spritz with olive
oil spray.

3 When all of the mixture has been formed, bake until golden and crusty,
20 to 25 minutes. Drizzle sauce decoratively onto 6 small plates and unmold
the timbales on top. Garnish with sage.

4 **To make the red wine sauce:** Bring the wine, 1 cup water, mushrooms,
tomatoes, and bay leaf to a boil in a saucepan over high heat. Simmer for
20 minutes. The liquid should reduce to ¾ cup. Strain and return to pan.
Mix the cornstarch and 1 tablespoon of water in a cup, then whisk it into the
saucepan, cooking until thick and clear. Stir in agave syrup and season with
salt to finish.

THAI OMELETS

with CABBAGE *and* TOFU

SERVES 4

Some Thai restaurants will make an omelet and the result is all mixed together so that it's really more like a frittata with veggies. Here's a pretty, folded omelette, stuffed with Thai spiced tofu and veggies and a tasty sauce, and with far less oil than the restaurant version.

INGREDIENTS

4 TEASPOONS PEANUT OIL

½ PACKAGE FIRM TOFU,
drained and pressed

¼ TEASPOON SALT

2 LARGE RED FRESNO
CHILES *or* JALAPEÑOS,
chopped

4 TABLESPOONS SOY SAUCE

1 SMALL CARROT,
finely julienned

2 CUPS CHOPPED CABBAGE

1 TABLESPOON CHOPPED FRESH GINGER

2 LARGE SCALLIONS,
sliced diagonally

1 LARGE TOMATO,
DICED

½ CUP HOLY BASIL,
julienned

8 LARGE EGGS

2 LARGE JALAPEÑOS,
minced

4 LARGE SHALLOTS,
thinly sliced (optional)

BOTTLED SWEET CHILI SAUCE

BOTTLED SRIRACHA SAUCE

1 Heat a wok over high heat until hot. Add 1 teaspoon peanut oil, swirl to coat the pan, then crumble in the tofu and add the salt. Stir-fry, scraping the pan. When the tofu is browned and firm, add the chiles and the 2 tablespoons of soy sauce, and stir well. Add the carrot, cabbage, ginger, scallions, and tomato and stir-fry until the cabbage is crisp-tender. Remove from the heat, stir in the basil, and keep warm.

2 In a medium bowl, whisk the eggs, the remaining 2 tablespoons soy sauce, and the jalapeños. Over medium heat, sauté the shallots (if using) in 1 teaspoon of the peanut oil until browned and soft, and add it to the egg mixture. Heat an 8-inch sauté pan over high heat and add one quarter of the remaining peanut oil, tilting pan to coat. Reduce heat to medium, pour in one-quarter of the eggs, tilting the pan to coat, and cook until just firm. Slide the eggs onto a plate, place the skillet on top, and flip the omelet back into the pan. Cook for about 1 minute. Transfer to a plate, cover loosely to keep warm, and continue with the remaining omelets. Fill the bottom half of the omelets with the stir-fry mixture and fold over to cover. Serve warm with the bottled sauces.

BÀNH MI SANDWICH

with PICKLED DAIKON *and* CARROTS

MAKES 4 SANDWICHES

The bành mi is a Vietnamese fusion, originating from the time when the French arrived in Vietnam and brought their baguettes with them. The sandwich is a delightful combination of the fresh, sweet, and sour flavors of Vietnamese salads, plus the pleasant contrast of a warm filling with cool vegetables. The mushroom pâté is not required, but it adds another note to the symphony in your mouth.

INGREDIENTS

¼ CUP PLUS 1 TABLESPOON
DRIED CANE JUICE

½ CUP RICE VINEGAR

¼ TEASPOON SALT

4 SLICES RED ONION

1 CUP SHREDDED DAIKON

½ CUP SHREDDED CARROT

2 TEASPOONS CANOLA OIL

2 LARGE SHALLOTS,
chopped

5 CLOVES GARLIC,
chopped

1 TABLESPOON CHOPPED FRESH GINGER

2 TABLESPOONS SOY SAUCE

1 TEASPOON CHINESE FIVE-SPICE POWDER

8 OUNCES SEITAN,
drained and sliced

FOUR 6-INCH BAGUETTE SECTIONS,
split (buy the widest baguettes available)

4 TABLESPOONS MAYONNAISE

8 SLICES CUCUMBER

8 SLICES VEGETARIAN MUSHROOM PÂTÉ,
or MUSHROOM PÂTÉ DE CAMPAGNE
WITH COGNAC AND PISTACHIOS,
page 25 (optional)

CHILI SAUCE

1 In a large bowl, mix the ¼ cup dried cane juice, the rice vinegar, and salt. Stir in the onion, daikon, and carrot. Let stand until ready to serve.

2 Heat a wok or cast-iron skillet over high heat. Add the oil, then add the shallots, garlic, and ginger and stir for a few seconds. Add the soy sauce, five-spice powder, the remaining 1 tablespoon dried cane juice and stir. Add the seitan and cook, stirring, until the liquids are absorbed. Remove from the heat.

3 Preheat the broiler. Pull out a bit of the insides of each baguette section to make room for the filling. Spread 1 tablespoon of mayonnaise on each baguette, then broil them 4 inches from the heat, until the mayonnaise is bubbly. Stuff each baguette with the seitan filling, cucumber slices, pâté (if using), and the daikon mixture. Add some chili sauce and serve hot.

MAC AND CHEESE

with HIDDEN VEGGIES

MAKES ABOUT 8 CUPS / SERVES 6

"Hiding the veggies" is one way to put extra vegetables into a familiar dish and still make something really tasty. If your kids are completely veggie averse, you can leave out the peas, and serve the macaroni in a bowl so it is segregated from any visible vegetable presence.

INGREDIENTS

1½ CUPS *(5 ounces)* CHOPPED CAULIFLOWER

2 MEDIUM CARROTS, *sliced*

1¼ CUPS BUTTERMILK

2½ CUPS *(or 6 ounces)* SHREDDED CHEDDAR CHEESE

2 TABLESPOONS BLUE CHEESE

¼ CUP SHREDDED PARMESAN CHEESE

½ TEASPOON SALT

3 CUPS MACARONI

1 CUP FROZEN PEAS *or* EDAMAME

½ CUP PANKO BREADCRUMBS

1 Put a pot of water on to boil for the macaroni. Steam the cauliflower and carrots until very soft, about 10 minutes. Purée the hot vegetables in a blender, then gradually add the buttermilk, puréeing until smooth. Add 2 cups of the cheddar cheese, the blue cheese, Parmesan, and salt and purée.

2 Cook the macaroni according to package directions. Add the peas at the last minute, just to thaw in the boiling water. Drain and shake thoroughly to dry. Put the pasta and peas back in the pot and stir in the sauce. In a small bowl, mix the remaining ½ cup cheddar with the breadcrumbs.

3 Preheat the oven to 400°F. Put the pasta and sauce in a 2-quart casserole, top with the crumb mixture, and bake until bubbly and crusty, 25 to 30 minutes. Serve hot.

EASY TOFU SCRAMBLE

with CORN, CILANTRO, *and* TOASTED PUMPKINSEEDS

MAKES ABOUT 3 CUPS / SERVES 2 TO 3

The humble tofu scramble has served vegetarians well: It's ever flexible and easy to make. Try this Southwestern-flavored one with crunchy pepitas and corn chips. Ovo-lactos can add an egg to the mixture before scrambling.

INGREDIENTS

10 OUNCES EXTRA-FIRM TOFU,
drained and pressed

2 to 3 BIG EARS SWEET CORN,
kernels removed
(or 2 cups canned)

2 LARGE SCALLIONS,
slivered

2 CUPS CHERRY TOMATOES,
halved and squeezed to remove extra juice

3 CLOVES GARLIC,
pressed

1 TABLESPOON NUTRITIONAL YEAST

1 TEASPOON CUMIN

1 TEASPOON CHILI POWDER

½ TEASPOON DRIED OREGANO

1 PINCH SAFFRON

1 WHOLE LIME,
zested and quartered

1 TEASPOON SALT

½ CUP PUMPKINSEEDS

OLIVE OIL SPRAY

½ CUP CHOPPED CILANTRO

4 CUPS CORN CHIPS

TABASCO SAUCE

1 In a large bowl, crush the tofu with your hands. Mix in the corn, scallions, tomatoes, garlic, yeast, cumin, chili powder, oregano, saffron, lime zest, and salt. Set aside.

2 Place the pumpkinseeds in a large cast-iron or nonstick skillet over high heat. Shaking the pan, toast the pumpkinseeds until they pop and begin turning darker. Remove them from the heat and pour them onto a plate.

3 Wipe the pan with a paper towel, then coat generously with olive oil spray. Add the tofu mixture and stir-fry over high heat. When the tofu is golden brown and dry, add the cilantro, stir for 1 minute, and remove from the heat. Divide the tofu among 2 or 3 plates.

4 Serve topped with pumpkinseeds, a handful of corn chips, and the lime quarters, and pass around the Tabasco at the table.

TOFU-CABBAGE KARHI

in CREAMY BUTTERMILK–GARBANZO FLOUR SAUCE

MAKES ABOUT 5 CUPS / SERVES 4

The garbanzo flour used to thicken this sauce is both deliciously nutty and nutritious. The ghee called for is clarified butter, which can take higher heat than butter. If you don't use ghee, use canola oil.

INGREDIENTS

1 PACKAGE FIRM TOFU,
drained and pressed

2 TABLESPOONS GHEE

2 TEASPOONS CUMIN SEEDS

2 TEASPOONS BLACK MUSTARD SEEDS

1 MEDIUM SHALLOT,
chopped

1 SMALL ZUCCHINI,
julienned

6 OUNCES *(or 2 cups)* CAULIFLOWER FLORETS

2 LARGE RED JALAPEÑOS,
chopped

1 TABLESPOON CHOPPED FRESH GINGER

2 CUPS BUTTERMILK

½ CUP GARBANZO FLOUR

1 CUP VEGETABLE STOCK

1 TEASPOON TURMERIC

2 TEASPOONS CORIANDER

1 TEASPOON CHILI POWDER

1 TEASPOON SALT

1 TABLESPOON BROWN SUGAR

½ TEASPOON GARAM MASALA

1 TABLESPOON LEMON JUICE

½ CUP CHOPPED CILANTRO

1 CUP BROWN JASMINE RICE
or WHOLE WHEAT CHAPATIS,
cooked

1 Cube the tofu and set aside. Place a large cast-iron skillet over high heat and, when hot, add the ghee. Add cumin and mustard seeds and the shallot, and stir. Add the tofu to the pan and cook until golden on each side, then turn over. Add zucchini, cauliflower, jalapeños, and ginger and stir, cooking until the vegetables are slightly softened and golden in spots.

2 In a large mixing bowl, whisk ½ cup of the buttermilk into the garbanzo flour to make a paste, then gradually whisk in the rest of the buttermilk. Whisk in the vegetable stock, turmeric, coriander, and chili powder. Pour the mixture into the pan of sautéing vegetables and tofu. Bring to a simmer, stirring, and cook over low heat for 20 to 30 minutes, adding water or stock if the sauce becomes too thick. Add the salt and brown sugar and stir well.

3 Just before serving, stir in the garam masala and lemon juice and sprinkle with the cilantro. Serve over rice.

TOFU TRIANGLES
STUFFED *with* SHIITAKES *in* MUSHROOM BROTH

SERVES 4

The architectural look of the tofu triangles, spiking up from a bowl of savory broth and colorful veggies, will impress your most discriminating friends. The eggs make a lovely golden coating and give the stuffing extra body, but vegans can simply omit them and instead use additional cornstarch and take extra care when searing the filling in the triangles.

INGREDIENTS

MUSHROOM BROTH

1 CUP DRIED MUSHROOMS,
rinsed

2 STALKS CELERY

STEMS FROM 8 OUNCES FRESH SHIITAKE MUSHROOMS,
caps reserved for triangles

TOFU TRIANGLES

8 OUNCES FRESH SHIITAKE MUSHROOMS,
stems removed but reserved for the broth

3 TEASPOONS DARK SESAME OIL

1 TABLESPOON MINCED FRESH GINGER

¼ CUP CHOPPED FRESH BASIL

1 TABLESPOON RICE WINE

1 TABLESPOON SOY SAUCE

1 EGG,
divided

2 TEASPOONS CORNSTARCH

½ TEASPOON SALT

2 PACKAGES EXTRA-FIRM TOFU,
drained and pressed

2 TABLESPOONS OIL

2 TABLESPOONS VEGETARIAN OYSTER SAUCE

2 TABLESPOONS SOY SAUCE

⅛ TEASPOON WHITE PEPPER

ONE 8-OUNCE CAN SLICED BAMBOO SHOOTS

1 MEDIUM CARROT,
julienned

1 CUP SNOW PEAS,
slivered

LONG-GRAIN BROWN RICE,
cooked

1 To make the broth: Put the dried mushrooms, celery, and 5 cups water in a 4-quart pot over high heat, bring to a boil, then reduce to a gentle simmer. As you prepare the shiitakes for the filling, put the stems in the simmering stock (along with any trimmings from the ginger and carrot). When the broth is fragrant and golden in hue, about 30 minutes, strain out the solids, leaving behind the last bit of liquid if it is gritty.

2 To make the triangles: Finely mince the shiitake caps and sauté them in the 1 teaspoon sesame oil until limp and dry, then add the ginger and cook for 1 minute. Let cool and stir in the basil, rice wine, soy sauce, 1 tablespoon of the egg white (reserve the rest), cornstarch, and salt. Cut the tofu blocks in half diagonally to form triangles, then use a paring knife to slice parallel to the sides to create a hollow pocket. Scoop out the inner tofu with a spoon. Mash the scooped-out tofu and mix it with the filling. Stuff the mushroom mixture inside the tofu pockets, carefully supporting the walls with your hands so they don't crumble. Smooth the outside surface with the back of a wet spoon. Chill the triangles on their sides until time to cook.

3 In a flat-bottomed small container, whisk the remaining egg white with the egg yolk. Dip the stuffed side of each tofu slice in the egg, then roll the rest in the egg. Heat the 2 tablespoons of oil over medium-high heat and fry the tofu, filling-side down, for about 2 minutes. When that side is sealed, turn and brown the remaining sides until golden.

4 In a 4-quart pot over medium-low heat, simmer the Mushroom Broth with the oyster sauce, soy sauce, 2 teaspoons sesame oil, and white pepper. When the tofu is browned, transfer the triangles to the stock and simmer very gently for 10 minutes. Add the vegetables and simmer until they are crisp-tender, about 2 minutes. Serve with the hot rice to soak up the broth.

GARBANZO CHOLE

with SAFFRON RICE

SERVES 4

The long tradition of vegetarianism in India has brought us incredibly sophisticated cuisine, redolent of spices and herbs. This easy version of chole employs the convenience of canned beans, but if you cook your own, add a black teabag to the simmering liquids for the traditional flavor and color.

INGREDIENTS

2 SMALL ONIONS,
peeled and chopped (2 cups)

2 MEDIUM JALAPEÑOS,
seeded

1-INCH PIECE FRESH GINGER,
peeled and sliced

3 CLOVES GARLIC,
peeled

1 CUP CANNED TOMATO SAUCE

1 TEASPOON VEGAN WORCESTERSHIRE SAUCE

1 TABLESPOON CANOLA OIL *or* GHEE

1½ CUPS CAULIFLOWER FLORETS

2 TEASPOONS GROUND CUMIN

½ TEASPOON GROUND TURMERIC

2 TEASPOONS GROUND CORIANDER

1 TEASPOON BROWN SUGAR

½ TEASPOON SALT

ONE 15-OUNCE CAN GARBANZO BEANS,
drained

¼ CUP CHOPPED CILANTRO

RICE

1 PINCH SAFFRON,
crumbled

1 CUP BASMATI RICE, BROWN *or* WHITE

½ TEASPOON SALT

1 Chop the onions and put half of them in a blender. Reserve the rest. Into the blender add the jalapeños, ginger, and garlic and process until finely minced. Add the tomato sauce and Worcestershire sauce and purée.

2 Heat a large cast-iron skillet over high heat. When hot, add the canola oil, then the reserved onions and the cauliflower. Cook until the onions are soft and golden, about 5 minutes. Add the cumin, turmeric, and coriander and stir until the spices are fragrant. Add the tomato mixture from the blender, the brown sugar, salt, garbanzo beans, and 1 cup water and bring to a simmer. Simmer, stirring often, until thick. Add cilantro just before serving over the hot rice.

3 **To make the rice:** Put the crumbled saffron in a 1-quart saucepan and heat over medium heat to toast. Add 1 ½ cups (2 cups if cooking with brown rice) water and bring to a boil, then add the rice and salt and return to a boil. Reduce the heat and simmer for 15 minutes for white rice (35 to 40 for brown).

CHAPTER 5

DESSERTS

WHEN IT COMES TO DESSERTS, OVO-LACTOS HAVE PLENTY OF OPTIONS. Bakeries crank out glorious butter- and egg-filled treats, and recipes are easy to come by. That's why all of these recipes are vegan. Conventional bakers are baffled when asked to make things rich without butter, flaky without lard, or fluffy without eggs. Vegans are seldom asked to bring dessert, for fear that a cake-shaped doorstop might be presented to the cowering crowd. It was with this bias in mind that I set out to make decadent, luscious, beautiful vegan desserts for this book.

When it is time to celebrate, vegans want show-stopping desserts just as much as the next guy or gal. These treats can compete with anything you see in the pages of cooking magazines or on restaurant menus.

To make great desserts without the usual animal products, it just takes a little chemistry. In many of these recipes, butter has been replaced by coconut oil, another fat that stays solid when cold and can be used to create flakiness in pastries. Because it has the unique characteristic of melting at 70°F, it will be solid in the refrigerator, or a cold room, and recipes specify whether it should be solid or liquid. For an oil with a buttery flavor, cold-pressed corn oil is used. Coconut milk is the vegan answer to cream. Tofu is used judiciously for creamy fillings, and rice milk provides moisture. Ground flaxseeds can even stand in for eggs, when mixed with water. Instead of white sugar, dried cane juice, raw sugar, maple syrup, and other vegan sweeteners give the desserts all the sweetness they need. Eggless and dairyless doesn't mean flavorless.

FUDGY MACADAMIA-RAISIN BROWNIES

MAKES ABOUT 16 BIG BROWNIES

Fruity, nutty, and dense, these brownies are a treat, with or without the topping. The hint of coconut flavor in the oil marries well with vanilla, macadamias, and, of course, chocolate, chocolate, chocolate!

INGREDIENTS

VEGETABLE OIL SPRAY

2 OUNCES UNSWEETENED CHOCOLATE,
chopped

½ CUP COCONUT OIL

2 CUPS LIGHT DRIED CANE JUICE

ONE 4-OUNCE JAR PRUNE-OATMEAL BABY FOOD

2 TEASPOONS VANILLA EXTRACT

3/4 CUP RICE MILK

¼ CUP WHOLE FLAXSEEDS,
ground

½ CUP WHOLE WHEAT PASTRY FLOUR

1 CUP UNBLEACHED FLOUR

¾ CUP COCOA

½ TEASPOON SALT

½ TEASPOON BAKING POWDER

¼ TEASPOON BAKING SODA

1 CUP MACADAMIA NUTS,
coarsely chopped

1 CUP RAISINS

TOPPING

½ CUP COCONUT OIL

2½ CUPS ORGANIC POWDERED SUGAR

1 TEASPOON VANILLA

5 TO 6 TABLESPOONS RICE MILK

2 OUNCES SEMISWEET CHOCOLATE,
chopped

1 Preheat the oven to 350°F. Coat a 9-inch-square baking pan with vegetable oil spray.

2 In a double boiler or in the microwave, melt the chocolate with the coconut oil. Stir until it is completely smooth, then take it off the heat. Add the cane juice to the chocolate mixture and mix thoroughly. When well combined, add the prune-oatmeal mixture and vanilla and beat to combine. In a cup, mix the rice milk with the flaxseeds and add it to the chocolate mixture. Beat to mix thoroughly.

3 In another bowl, whisk both the flours, the cocoa, salt, baking powder, and baking soda. Stir it into the wet mixture just until moistened. Stir in the nuts and raisins.

4 Scrape the batter into the prepared pan and smooth the top. Bake until done around the edges but still moist in the middle, 40 to 55 minutes. Let cool completely before adding the topping and slicing into squares. Bring to room temperature before serving.

5 **To make the topping:** In a stand mixer or bowl, beat the coconut oil, powdered sugar, and vanilla. Then gradually add the rice milk a tablespoon at a time; after the first 3, a thick paste should form. Beat in the remaining rice milk until a stiff frosting is formed. Spread the frosting on the cold brownies. Melt the semisweet chocolate and drizzle it over the frosting decoratively. Chill until the chocolate is set, then slice.

SWEET POTATO SHORTCAKES

with CRANBERRY FILLING

MAKES 9 SHORTCAKES

{ Springtime gets the strawberry shortcakes, so why not have a winter shortcake? Here, cranberries are spiked with maple syrup, and shortcakes are laced with sweet potatoes. It's a great make-ahead dessert, just warm the shortcakes and cranberries before serving. }

INGREDIENTS

4 CUPS CRANBERRIES

1 CUP MAPLE SYRUP

1 CUP WHOLE WHEAT PASTRY FLOUR

1 CUP CAKE FLOUR

½ CUP DRIED CANE JUICE

2 TEASPOONS BAKING POWDER

½ TEASPOON BAKING SODA

½ TEASPOON SALT

½ CUP COCONUT OIL
or MARGARINE,
chilled and diced

¾ CUP SWEET POTATO,
puréed

¼ CUP SOY MILK *or* COCONUT MILK

1 TEASPOON VANILLA EXTRACT

½ CUP CHOPPED CRYSTALLIZED GINGER

10 TEASPOONS RAW SUGAR
(large crystals)

2 CUPS SOY *or*
OTHER VEGAN WHIPPED CREAM
or VANILLA YOGURT *or* ICE CREAM

1 In a 2-quart pot over high heat, bring the cranberries and maple syrup to a boil, then reduce the heat and simmer until thick, about 10 minutes. Let cool or chill.

2 Preheat the oven to 400°F. In a large bowl, whisk the pastry flour, cake flour, dried cane juice, baking powder, baking soda, and salt. Using a grater or pastry cutter, grate or cut in the coconut oil until it is the size of rice grains. In a small bowl, whisk the sweet potato, soy milk, and vanilla.

3 Stir the wet mixture into the dry until just mixed. Shape the dough into a 10-inch square about ¾ inch thick. Cut to make 9 squares. Sprinkle the tops with the crystallized ginger and raw sugar crystals, pressing to adhere. Use a metal spatula to transfer the shortcakes to a dry baking sheet. Bake for 5 minutes.

4 Let the shortcakes cool for 5 minutes, then split and fill them with the cranberry mixture and top with the vegan whipped cream or an alternative topping, such as yogurt or ice cream.

APPLE STREUSEL CAKE

SERVES 10

Two different oils do two different jobs here. Real cold-pressed corn oil tastes buttery, and coconut oil gives the streusel the same texture as real butter would. The crunchy almond topping will have your guests coming back for more.

INGREDIENTS

STREUSEL

½ CUP WHOLE WHEAT PASTRY FLOUR
½ CUP WHOLE ALMONDS
1½ TEASPOONS CINNAMON
¼ CUP BROWN SUGAR
¼ CUP COCONUT OIL,
melted if necessary

CAKE

VEGETABLE OIL *or* SPRAY
1 CUP UNBLEACHED FLOUR
1 CUP WHOLE WHEAT PASTRY FLOUR
1 CUP DRIED CANE JUICE
1 TEASPOON BAKING POWDER
½ TEASPOON BAKING SODA
¼ TEASPOON SALT
1 TABLESPOON LEMON ZEST
¼ CUP COLD-PRESSED CORN OIL
1 CUP SOY MILK *or* RICE MILK
1 TEASPOON VANILLA
½ TEASPOON ALMOND EXTRACT
3 TABLESPOONS LEMON JUICE
3 CUPS CHOPPED GRANNY SMITH APPLE

1 To make the streusel: In a food processor, combine the whole wheat pastry flour, almonds, cinnamon, brown sugar, and liquid coconut oil. Process until the nuts are coarsely chopped and the mixture is well blended. Scrape out into a small bowl and chill.

2 To make the cake: Preheat the oven to 350°F. Coat a 9-inch-square baking pan with vegetable oil spray. In a large bowl, combine both the flours, dried cane juice, baking powder, baking soda, salt, and lemon zest, and mix well.

3 In a large glass measuring cup, measure the corn oil, add the soy milk, then whisk in the vanilla, almond extract, and lemon juice. Stir the wet mixture into the dry until well combined, then fold in the apples. Scrape the mixture into the prepared baking pan and top with the streusel.

4 Bake until a toothpick inserted into the center of the cake comes out with no wet batter attached, 45 to 50 minutes. Let cool in the pan for 10 minutes before slicing.

CHOCOLATE KAHLÚA CAKE

with MOCHA FILLING *and* GANACHE

SERVES 8

This rich, dark chocolate cake is so delicious, nobody will suspect that it is vegan. It's been scaled down to loaf size, so that you don't have to make a full-on layer cake to enjoy it. For special occasions, place red nasturtium flowers on top of each slice for a burst of color.

INGREDIENTS

MOCHA FILLING

5.5 OUNCES SILKEN TOFU,
drained

3 OUNCES SEMISWEET CHOCOLATE

¼ CUP AGAVE SYRUP

GANACHE

3 OUNCES SEMISWEET CHOCOLATE,
chopped

3 TABLESPOONS SOY MILK *or* COCONUT MILK

2 TABLESPOONS KAHLÚA

CAKE

1¼ CUPS UNBLEACHED FLOUR

¼ CUP COCOA,
sifted

1 TEASPOON BAKING POWDER

1 TEASPOON BAKING SODA

½ TEASPOON SALT

1 OUNCE SEMISWEET CHOCOLATE,
chopped

¼ CUP CANOLA OIL

½ CUP AGAVE SYRUP

1 CUP SOY MILK *or* COCONUT MILK

1 TEASPOON VANILLA EXTRACT

1 TEASPOON RICE VINEGAR

1 TABLESPOON KAHLÚA

8 SMALL EDIBLE FLOWERS

1 To make the filling: In a food processor, purée the tofu until smooth. Melt the chocolate over a double boiler or in the microwave. Add the agave and chocolate to the tofu and purée immediately. Set aside.

2 To make the ganache: In a double boiler or in the microwave, melt the chocolate with the soy milk. Stir until smooth, then stir in the Kahlúa. Set aside.

3 To make the cake: Preheat the oven to 350°F. Grease a 6-cup loaf pan, preferably a metal one. In a large bowl, whisk the flour, cocoa, baking powder, baking soda, and salt. In a medium bowl set over a pot of barely simmering water, melt the chocolate with the canola oil. Remove from the heat and stir until smooth, then whisk in the agave syrup. In another bowl, stir together the soy milk, vanilla, vinegar, and Kahlúa, then stir it into the chocolate mixture. Stir the wet mixture into the dry, then scrape the batter into the prepared pan.

4 Bake until a toothpick inserted into the center of the loaf comes out with only moist crumbs attached, 35 to 40 minutes. Remove the pan and place it on a cooling rack for 15 minutes, then gently invert the loaf onto the rack to cool completely.

5 Using a serrated knife, carefully slice the cake into 3 even layers. Place the top layer, top-side down, on a platter or cake plate. Spread it with half of the filling. Top with the second layer and spread the remaining filling on it. Top with the final layer and use a spatula to smooth the filling on the sides so that it is flush with the cake layers, making a smooth, flat surface for the ganache.

6 Spread the ganache on the top and sides of the cake. If desired, place edible flowers in a row down the top of the cake, 1 per slice. Refrigerate until ready to serve.

CHOCOLATE CREAM AND RASPBERRY NAPOLEONS

with WALNUTS

SERVES 5

In Paris, pastry shops have cases lined with sparkling fruit tarts, rich chocolate cakes, and decadent Napoleons just like this one, but made with cream and butter. You will be amazed at how rich and crunchy these vegan treats are. Your guests will never know.

INGREDIENTS

4 SHEETS PHYLLO,
thawed overnight in the refrigerator

¼ CUP COCONUT OIL,
melted

½ CUP TURBINADO SUGAR

4 TABLESPOONS FINELY CHOPPED WALNUTS

½ CUP DRIED CANE JUICE

1½ CUPS COCONUT MILK

1 CUP SOY CREAMER

5 TABLESPOONS CORNSTARCH

1 TABLESPOON VANILLA EXTRACT

1 PINCH SALT

3 OUNCES SEMISWEET CHOCOLATE,
finely chopped

2 CUPS FRESH RASPBERRIES,
washed and dried

1 Preheat the oven to 350°F. Place the phyllo on the counter, cover with plastic wrap, and then put a barely damp towel over that, making sure the phyllo is not exposed to air. Prepare two sheet pans with parchment paper and two more pans that fit inside the first two. Place 1 sheet of phyllo on the counter and brush lightly with some melted coconut oil, then sprinkle the phyllo with 2 tablespoons of the sugar and 1 tablespoon of walnuts. Repeat with remaining sheets. Cut the sheets in half and move 1 stack on top of the other, creating a stack 8 sheets thick. Cut the rectangle in 4 strips one way, then the other, making 16 pieces. Transfer to the baking sheets with parchment—don't worry if they are close, but they should not be touching. Place the empty baking sheets on top of the phyllo to hold it flat, and bake until golden and crisp, 13 to 15 minutes. Let cool. (They can be stored in an airtight container for up to 1 week.)

....

2 In a medium saucepan over medium-high heat, whisk the dried cane juice, coconut milk, and ½ cup of the soy creamer. Put the remaining creamer into a cup and whisk in the cornstarch. Bring the coconut milk mixture to a simmer and add the vanilla and salt. Whisk in the cornstarch slurry and cook until thickened and glossy. Remove from the heat and stir in the chocolate. Let stand for 2 minutes, then stir until completely melted and smooth. Scrape the mixture into a bowl and cover with plastic wrap touching the surface and chill completely.

....

3 Set aside 15 nice raspberries for the top garnish. Transfer the pudding to a large piping bag with a large fluted tip. Place 5 of the phyllo rectangles on small plates or one large platter and pipe 3 tablespoons of the pudding onto each phyllo. Insert some raspberries into the chocolate and top with another phyllo rectangle. Repeat, then top each final phyllo with a piped dab of pudding and push 3 reserved raspberries onto each. Discard the extra phyllo rectangle. Serve within 24 hours.

LITTLE MANGO UPSIDE-DOWN CAKES

MAKES 5 CAKES

{ These divine little cakes are mostly mango—with a few bites of tender cake. Laced with lime zest and a hint of Chinese five-spice powder, this is a great dessert to serve with Asian food. }

INGREDIENTS

3 TABLESPOONS COCONUT OIL,
2 tablespoons softened

3 TABLESPOONS PLUS ½ CUP PALM
or RAW SUGAR

1 TEASPOON LIME ZEST

2 MEDIUM MANGOES

¾ CUP UNBLEACHED FLOUR

¼ TEASPOON BAKING SODA

¼ TEASPOON SALT

⅛ TEASPOON CHINESE FIVE-SPICE POWDER

½ CUP COCONUT MILK

1 TABLESPOON LIME JUICE

1 Preheat the oven to 350°F. Use 1 teaspoon of the unsoftened coconut oil to coat the bottoms and sides of five 8-ounce ramekins. Mix another 2 teaspoons of unsoftened coconut oil with the 3 tablespoons palm sugar and the lime zest and divide the mixture among the ramekins.

2 Peel the mangoes, then slice each rounded side off the pit. Slicing across the grain, cut the mango into ¼-inch-thick pieces, keeping the fruit intact. Fan about a third of a mango (rounded-side down) in each ramekin.

3 In a small bowl, whisk together the flour, baking soda, salt, and five-spice powder. In a stand mixer or with a handheld mixer, beat the 2 tablespoons softened coconut oil and palm sugar until fluffy. Beat in the coconut milk and lime juice, then add the dry ingredients and beat to blend. Divide the batter among the prepared ramekins, using wet fingers to distribute the mixture evenly over the fruit.

4 Bake until a toothpick inserted in the center comes out clean, 25 to 35 minutes. Let cool on a rack for 5 minutes. Run a paring knife around the edges of the cakes to loosen. Place a small plate over each cup and carefully flip the cake onto the plate. Pull the ramekin off and use the paring knife to put any fruit that sticks to the ramekin back onto the cake. Serve warm or cool.

MAPLE-OAT CHOCOLATE CHIP COOKIES

with WALNUTS *and* CRAISINS

MAKES ABOUT 14 BIG COOKIES

A cookie like this, loaded with crunchy, chewy, chocolaty goodness, is the perfect treat. You will enjoy every bite while filling up on whole grains and healthful stuff.

INGREDIENTS

1½ CUPS OLD-FASHIONED ROLLED OATS

1½ CUPS WHOLE WHEAT PASTRY FLOUR

¾ TEASPOON BAKING SODA

¼ TEASPOON SALT

6 TABLESPOONS COLD-PRESSED CORN OIL

¾ CUP PURE MAPLE SYRUP
(grade B)

1 TEASPOON VANILLA EXTRACT

1 CUP CHOCOLATE CHIPS

½ CUP COARSELY CHOPPED WALNUTS

½ CUP CRAISINS

1 Preheat the oven to 350°F. Line a large baking sheet with parchment paper or a silpat.

2 In a large bowl, stir together the oats, flour, baking soda, and salt. In a medium bowl, stir the oil, maple syrup, and vanilla. Stir the wet ingredients into the dry ingredients, then stir in the chocolate chips, walnuts, and craisins.

3 Scoop ¼-cup portions of dough and place on a prepared baking sheet. With wet hands, flatten the dough to ¾ inch thick and press in any stray chunks. Bake for 8 minutes, turn, and bake for 8 minutes more. Let cool on the pan for 5 minutes, then transfer to racks. Store in zip-top bags or tightly wrapped for up to a week.

PECAN SHORTBREAD

with PISTACHIO GELATO *and* POACHED PEARS

SERVES 6

Fine restaurants these days have pastry chefs designing desserts with at least three components, so that the diner gets lots of tastes and textures for maximum enjoyment. Vegans get the option here of making a composed plate with three nut-flavored treats, or just make any one of them to enjoy on their own.

INGREDIENTS

PISTACHIO GELATO

1½ CUPS SHELLED PISTACHIOS

½ CUP DRIED CANE JUICE

2 CUPS RICE MILK
(not soy milk)

PECAN SHORTBREAD

1½ CUPS CAKE FLOUR

½ CUP POWDERED SUGAR

¼ TEASPOON SALT

1½ CUPS GROUND PECANS

6 TABLESPOONS COCONUT OIL

2 TABLESPOONS COLD-PRESSED CORN OIL

1 TEASPOON VANILLA EXTRACT

2 TABLESPOONS TURBINADO SUGAR
(large crystals)

POACHED PEARS

6 SMALL BOSC PEARS,
peeled

2 CUPS WHITE GRAPE JUICE

¼ CUP DRIED CANE JUICE

½ CUP FRANGELICO HAZELNUT LIQUEUR

8 TOASTED HAZELNUTS,
finely chopped

1 **To make the gelato:** In a blender, purée the pistachios, cane juice, and rice milk until as finely minced as possible. Transfer to a container and refrigerate overnight. The next day, pour it through a fine-mesh strainer, pressing with a rubber spatula to extract all the liquids. Discard the solids. Freeze in an ice cream machine, according to the manufacturer's directions.

2 **To make the shortbread:** In a large bowl, sift together the cake flour, powdered sugar, and salt. Stir in the pecans. Melt the coconut oil with the corn oil, if necessary, in a small pan or the microwave. Stir in the vanilla and mix the oils into the dry mixture. Roll the dough into a cyclinder 2 inches across on a piece of plastic wrap about 10 inches long. Wrap the dough with the plastic and refrigerate for at least 30 minutes.

3 Preheat the oven to 350°F. Slice the chilled dough into 4 segments, then cut each of those into 3 slices. Place the disks onto an ungreased baking sheet, sprinkle with the turbinado sugar, and bake until golden around the edges, about 18 minutes. Let cool on the pan for 5 minutes, then transfer to a rack to cool completely.

4 **To make poached pears:** Carefully peel the pears whole, leaving the stems. In a 4-quart saucepan, mix the grape juice, dried cane juice, and Frangelico. Add the pears and bring to a boil. Poach, turning gently, for about 30 minutes. When the pears are tender, remove them with a slotted spoon. Continue boiling the liquids until reduced to a thick syrup. As the pears cool, pour the syrup over them.

5 To serve, drizzle some of the pear syrup decoratively onto a small plate, and arrange a pear, 2 cookies, and ⅓ cup of the gelato. Sprinkle the pear with the chopped hazelnuts.

SWEET COCONUT EMPANADITAS
with CARAMEL SAUCE

MAKES 12 EMPANADITAS

A vegan caramel sauce and a creamy, crunchy pastry? Yes, and the skills required are not advanced. Coconut oil takes the place of shortening, and a caramel sauce made with coconut milk is to die for.

INGREDIENTS

CARAMEL SAUCE

¾ CUP DRIED CANE JUICE
½ CUP COCONUT MILK
1 PINCH SALT

FILLING

1 CUP COCONUT MILK
¼ CUP ORGANIC BROWN SUGAR
1 PINCH SALT
2 TABLESPOONS CORNSTARCH
¾ CUP SWEETENED COCONUT FLAKES, *toasted*
1 TEASPOON VANILLA EXTRACT

CRUST

1½ CUPS UNBLEACHED FLOUR
¼ CUP SUGAR
½ TEASPOON SALT
½ CUP COCONUT OIL, *melted and chilled*
12 TABLESPOONS ICE WATER
1 TEASPOON CINNAMON
2 TABLESPOONS DRIED CANE JUICE

1 To make the sauce: In a 2-quart saucepan over medium-high heat, combine the dried cane juice and ⅔ cup water. Stir until the dried cane juice is dissolved. Raise the heat to high but don't stir—just swirl the pan over the heat until the bubbling liquid turns from Champagne-colored to an amber-caramel tone. Remove the pan from the heat and immediately pour in the coconut milk (be careful not to let the liquid boil over). Put the pan back over the heat, stirring. Add the salt and cook over medium heat to dissolve all the sugar. When smooth, remove from the heat and transfer to a pouring cup.

2 To make the filling: In a small, heavy-bottomed saucepan over medium-high heat, combine the coconut milk, brown sugar, salt, and cornstarch. Bring to a simmer, whisking until thickened. Remove from the heat and scrape the mixture into a small bowl. Stir in coconut and vanilla. Cover with plastic wrap, pressing the wrap gently down onto the surface of the pudding. Chill for at least 30 minutes.

3 To make the crust: Preheat the oven to 400°F. In a large bowl, mix the flour, sugar, and salt. Using the big holes of a grater, grate the chilled coconut oil into the flour mixture. Toss to mix, then gradually stir in the ice water just until the dough can be pressed together to form a ball. Divide the dough into 6 pieces, then chill for 30 minutes.

4 Roll out each ball into a 6-inch-long oval, then cut it in half crosswise to make two pieces. Holding the dough in your palm, dampen half of the straight edge, then pull the other side around and seal them to make an open cone. Place 2 tablespoons of the filling into the cone, dampen the top, and press the dough together to make a three-sided pastry. Use a fork to seal the edge. Continue until all 12 are formed. Place them on a baking sheet, brush with water, and sprinkle with the cinnamon and dried cane juice. Bake until the bottoms are browned and the edges are crisp, 20 to 25 minutes.

5 Serve warm, drizzled with the sauce.

YUZU KANTEN AND MATCHA MOUSSE PARFAITS

with SEASONAL FRUIT

SERVES 6

Of course, no vegan dessert list would be complete without kanten, made with a seaweed-derived gelling agent called agar. It's also considered a diet aid, since it fills you up. This is a beautiful dessert, with tart orange kanten, sweet creamy mousse, and lots of the fruit of the moment. You can also just make kanten and even substitute lemon juice, and eat it plain for a simple snack.

INGREDIENTS

KANTEN

7 TABLESPOONS AGAR FLAKES

3 CUPS MANGO JUICE

½ CUP BOTTLED YUZU JUICE
or LEMON JUICE

3 CUPS FRESH SEASONAL FRUIT
*(berries, pears, peaches, mango, etc.)
washed and sliced, if necessary*

½ CUP DRIED CANE JUICE

½ TEASPOON VANILLA EXTRACT

MOUSSE

1 CUP COCONUT MILK

½ TEASPOON AGAR POWDER

½ CUP DRIED CANE JUICE

2 TABLESPOONS CORNSTARCH

2 TEASPOONS MATCHA POWDER

1 CUP RICE MILK

MINT SPRIGS FOR GARNISH
(optonal)

1 **To make the kanten:** In a medium saucepan over high heat, combine the agar flakes, mango, and yuzu juices, and let soak for 30 minutes. Bring to a boil, whisk, then turn off the heat and cover to soak for 30 minutes more. Set aside some fruit for garnish and divide the rest among 6 wine glasses or small bowls.

2 Over low heat, stir the mixture in the saucepan. Add the dried cane juice. Cook until the agar is dissolved, stirring often. Add the vanilla extract. Portion ½ cup of the mixture into each wineglass and chill until set.

3 **To make the mousse:** In a medium saucepan over medium heat, heat the coconut milk and agar powder with the cane juice, stirring to dissolve. When it starts to simmer, whisk the cornstarch and matcha together in a small cup, then whisk in a couple tablespoons of rice milk to make a paste. Gradually whisk in the rest of the rice milk until smooth. Whisk the mixture into the simmering liquid and cook until thickened, whisking continuously. Remove from the heat, let cool slightly, then portion about ⅓ cup on top of the kanten in each glass. Chill.

4 Serve garnished with the reserved fruit slices or berries and a mint sprig, if desired.

INDEX

TABLE OF EQUIVALENTS

The exact equivalents in the following tables have been rounded for convenience.

LIQUID/DRY MEASUREMENTS

U.S.	METRIC
¼ teaspoon	1.25 milliliters
½ teaspoon	2.5 milliliters
1 teaspoon	5 milliliters
1 tablespoon (3 teaspoons)	15 milliliters
1 fluid ounce (2 tablespoons)	30 milliliters
¼ cup	60 milliliters
⅓ cup	80 milliliters
½ cup	120 milliliters
1 cup	240 milliliters
1 pint (2 cups)	480 milliliters
1 quart (4 cups, 32 ounces)	960 milliliters
1 gallon (4 quarts)	3.84 liters
1 ounce (by weight)	28 grams
1 pound	448 grams
2.2 pounds	1 kilogram

LENGTHS

U.S.	METRIC
⅛ inch	3 millimeters
¼ inch	6 millimeters
½ inch	12 millimeters
1 inch	2.5 centimeters

OVEN TEMPERATURE

FAHRENHEIT	CELSIUS	GAS
250	120	½
275	140	1
300	150	2
325	160	3
350	180	4
375	190	5
400	200	6
425	220	7
450	230	8
475	240	9
500	260	10